The Sexual Purity Detox

Detoxifying Heart, Mind, and Body of Sexual Sin

Maretha Burkley

Dedication

At the tender age of about ten years old I had conversations with my mother that changed the trajectory of my life forever without her even knowing the impact those conversations were having. My mother would tell me stories about my grandmother in which she described my grandmother in such a way that I felt as if my grandmother was someone I had grown up with. My grandmother died when I was nine months old, but her faith helped raise me. I was very young when my mother told me about my grandmothers specific teaching that sex was for married people. I never forgot those words. Even before I found my way to Christ, the desire to wait until marriage to have sex was planted in my heart because of my grandmothers 'teachings. I have now been celibate for twenty-three years at the time of this writing. Hopefully at the time of you reading this I have crossed over to a beautiful and godly marriage with my physical husband, whoever that is. I would like to dedicate this book to my sweet, amazing, and admirable grandmother, *Bessie Lee Ramey*.

I thank my mother, *Rosalind*, for giving me the best she had as a mother and for passing on to me the lessons she learned from Bessie Lee.

Most importantly, I thank my Lord and savior *Jesus* for living for me, dying for me, and rising for me. I look forward to seeing you in Heaven!

Contents

Introduction

Why did God give me a body that wants sex now if he doesn't want me to have sex until marriage!? Most of us have asked God this question at some point while being single. Sexual desire can make us feel as if God is dangling a carrot in our faces. Sex is like the donuts that show up at the office every time you start a fast or a weight loss program. They are right there in front of you everywhere you look but you can't have them. Forgive me if those analogies are too honest, but the point I want to make is that I understand. I totally understand what you might be going through!

As a single woman who has been celibate for twenty-three years, I struggled for purity for many years. I have felt the deep darkness of hopelessness during times of feeling like I couldn't shake lust and I have stood on the mountain top of pride and arrogance when I felt that I had escaped the struggle that everyone else was having. I have felt like I hated being a sexual being all together at times when I couldn't reconcile the fact that God created me as a sexual being but then called me to live without sex until I am married. There was a time in my life when I was running to my doctor's office literally begging them to prescribe me something to take the internal desire for sex away. My doctors, yes "doctors" meaning plural! all told me that my issue was not one they could help and that they only help people who have the opposite issue. I just wanted to turn it off and make it go away so I could peacefully focus on my relationship with my Heavenly father. I know that many of you who are reading this have gone through similar struggles. I get you. I understand and that is why I have authored this book. I not only understand your struggle, but I also understand the power of God and his ability to give you victory.

One of the most common questions I have heard is "why did God not just wait to give me sexual desires when I get married if he wants me to be pure?". Understanding that we are created in perfection and that the enemy is constantly working to use our own perfect design against us is a challenge. As we read through this book, I hope that we will gain a greater understanding of the difference between design and desire. I hope that we will learn to discern the difference between the voice of a perfectly functioning body and the voice of the enemy begging and pleading for an opportunity to misuse God's creation. The way we will learn these very important things is by reading Gods' word and seeing how he calls us to sexual purity repeatedly throughout the bible. As we read through the scriptures in this book, I hope we hear God yearning for us to be set apart for him in our sexual purity.

There are some things that are going to be vital to us getting the most out of this book. One key thing is that we must commit to fasting and prayer. In this detox we will be fasting for twenty-one days. You will choose what you will fast from. Praying and fasting is going to be very helpful and powerful because lust is a struggle of the flesh. The flesh must be tamed and put in check if we want to overcome the act of sexual impurity and lusting. When we fast, we tell our body "No" and we train ourselves in self-control.

When Jesus was in the garden of Gethsemane, he confessed that the Spirit is willing, but the flesh is weak. Even though Jesus was perfect in Spirit he was living in a body of flesh that was still prone to temptation.

Let us look at (Matthew 26:39-41)

"Going a little farther, he fell with his face to the ground and prayed, "My Father, if it is possible, may this cup be taken from me. Yet not as I will, but as you will."

Then he returned to his disciples and found them sleeping. "Couldn't you men keep watch with me for one hour?" he asked Peter. "Watch and pray so that you will not fall into temptation. The spirit is willing, but the flesh is weak."

In the verse above we see that our perfect Jesus was not willing to sin in his Spirit, but in his flesh, he was still faced with temptation. When temptation comes to us, we must recognize that it is our flesh that is exposed to Satan, and he tries to appeal to it in order to reach us spiritually. Satan wanted to tempt Jesus into making a decision that would disrupt God's plan. Satan wanted to use Jesus' flesh against him. Satan has this same agenda with us too. He wants to use our own flesh against us. For this reason, it is important for us to understand and discern the difference between our willing spirits and our weak flesh just as Jesus did. It is also super important for us to fast as we are working to mature in resisting impurity and lust. Fasting sets aside our usual focus on pleasing the flesh, even in eating, for us to focus on pleasing God while we are fasting.

During this detox we will read and meditate on scriptures that speak about Gods' standard for purity and his call for us to control our bodies. Meditating on Gods' word daily will help us understand the presence of the enemy better and we will also gain a better understanding of the presence of God and his ability to bring us victory over temptation when we reach out to him through prayer and fasting.

In addition to committing to the fasting and prayer in this detox we must also commit to meditating on each daily meditation scripture which will equip us to stand against the enemy. When we meditate on the word of God, we are bringing it into memory so that we can have it readily available when Satan comes to tempt us. We recall that when Jesus was in the desert being tempted by Satan, he spoke the word of God against every temptation that Satan tried to trap him with. If we are going to be imitators of Christ, then we should pay close attention to how he lived his life and do likewise.

Let us look at (Matthew 4:2-7)

"After fasting forty days and forty nights, he was hungry. The tempter came to him and said, "If you are the Son of God, tell these stones to become bread."

Jesus answered, "It is written: 'Man shall not live on bread alone, but on every word that comes from the mouth of God."

Then the devil took him to the holy city and had him stand on the highest point of the temple. "If you are the Son of God," he said, "throw yourself down. For it is written:

"'He will command his angels concerning you,

and they will lift you up in their hands,

so that you will not strike your foot against a stone.'"

Jesus answered him, "It is also written: 'Do not put the Lord your God to the test."

In the passage listed above Jesus was ready with the word when Satan tried to come after him. Our commitment to daily meditation on the scriptures in this detox will help us be ready with the word as well. As we go through this detox, we will need to commit to every part of this detox in order to bring all the tools that God has given us into our fight against Satan and his goal of using our own beautifully designed bodies against us.

Another very important part of the detox that we must commit to is confession. The word of God tells us that for us to be forgiven of sin we must confess our sins and bring them into the light. The confession part of this detox is focused on bringing anything we have been hiding into the light so that we can move forward in this detox and begin our new walk-in purity with a clean slate. The focus of this part of the detox is not on creating a revolving door to giving in to lust and confessing afterwards. Sinning and confessing should not be an endless cycle that never leads us to true growth and repentance. True repentance is the aim, and God can give us the strength we need to repent.

I know that the thought of confessing sin can be terrifying to some people. As we get into the chapter on confession it is important that we decide to bear all and be humble in the eyes of God and not allow fear of what man will think keep us from confessing our sins. Satan wants to keep us in a secret tie with him, but God wants to set us free. Satan will cause us to condemn ourselves with guilt and shame if we allow him to convince us to hide our sin. Another danger of not exposing our sin is our conscience becoming desensitized leaving us numb to our sin and causing us to freely give in to lust and sexual sin even more. You are reading this book because you want to be free! Even if you are questioning whether you truly want to repent of sexual sin, the fact that you are reading this book speaks loudly and clearly of the fact that you want sexual purity. In order to be free, you will need to expose your sin and leave that secret connection you have to Satan. Don't let fear of the judgment of man or people keep you from being in the purity you desire in your relationship with God. Confess and let God cover you in your vulnerability.

Let us look at (1 John 1:10)

"If we confess our sins, he is faithful and just and will forgive us our sins and purify us from all unrighteousness.

If we claim we have not sinned, we make him out to be a liar and his word has no place in our lives."

The scripture listed above tells us why we need to humbly confess our sins. When we confess our sins, God is faithful, and He will forgive us for our sins. God wants to purify us from all our unrighteous ways and for him to do that we have to treat our sin as sin by confessing it. All sin is a big deal or Jesus would not have had to pay such a big price for it. We must not allow there to be any hidden and secret sin in our lives. This is why as part of this detox we must bring all our sins to the light and confess them. I will guide you through the confession part of this detox in chapter two.

Finally, we need to journal the journey. We must pull in the wisdom of writing to remember. The word of God being written has helped us to be able to read and refer to what we would otherwise forget if we didn't have it written down. We take note of what we go through and our growth so that we can have evidence to fight against the lies of the enemy. When we keep a journal of something it is a record of truth that can help keep us sober from lies about how well we're doing, and it also keeps us encouraged against lies about how we're not growing at all. In chapter one I explain more about the great benefits of keeping a journal and how vital daily journaling will be as we go through this detox journey.

The best way for us to start this detox is to read through the first six chapters thoroughly so that we understand the importance of holding fast to each part of this detox. These first six chapters are here to help us fully understand how this detox works and to prepare our mind so that we complete the full twenty-one days of this detox.

I hope and pray that the power of God will come over your heart, mind, soul, and body in way greater than you can ask, think or imagine. I pray that you find pleasure in purity as you seek God and his will during this detox. I pray that you overcome every scheme and trap that the enemy has set up against you in your purity and that you gain power and strength in resisting Satan in the face of temptation. Greater is He that is in you than he that is in the world! You are more than a conqueror. You will have victory in the name of Jesus! God did not call you into what is impossible. He called you and equipped you with everything you need for righteousness and godliness *(1 Peter 1:3 says, "his divine power, God has given us everything we need for living a godly life.")*. The enemy wants you to believe that purity is impossible. May God strengthen you and when you overcome make sure you turn back and strengthen your brothers and or sister. To God's glory!

Chapter One

Journaling Your Journey

"Journal writing, when it becomes a ritual for transformation, is not only life-changing but life-expanding."

JEN WILLIAMSON

The first thing we should address is how vital it is for us to journal our journey through this detox. Journaling is a wonderful way to process our current thoughts as we are meditating on the daily scripture readings. Writing down our thoughts is also a good way to keep a record of our progress as we grow in renewing our minds about sexual purity.

Keeping Your Journal Pure

The most important part of journaling is making sure that we are completely honest with ourselves as we write out our responses to the journal questions. It is easy to be tempted to write only what we feel comfortable seeing on the page. When we allow ourselves to be completely genuine and raw in our journal it will later serve as a great reminder of where God has brought us from. It will also be a great reference when and if we need to assess where we are in our journey to purity. Being honest and transparent in our journal will also keep our journal pure. Keeping our journal pure means keeping it free of any "non-truths" that can keep us in darkness. We don't want to contaminate our journal with anything that keeps us from seeing the truth. The truth is necessary for helping us grow spiritually. The bible says that Satan is the master of confusion and the father or lies. The enemy would love to hinder our growth through preventing us from getting in touch with our truth.

As you write down your answers to each of the daily questions and as you write out your temptations be specific and transparent so that way the enemy cannot keep you in the darkness of denial.

Reading through your journal after you have completed the purity detox can be very sobering and eye opening. Sometimes we don't really understand our thoughts and feelings while we are going through a struggle. Being able to look back over your notes and journal entries later will also help in your introspection about your struggles. My ultimate hope for you is that you will be able to celebrate your growth when you read through your journal after completing this detox.

Journaling will also help to make sure you are not just glossing over the scriptures that you are meditating on each day. Writing out what you learn from the scriptures will help you to pause and really process what you are reading in the word of God.

When we use a journal, it helps us see what we need from God more clearly. Being able to read our struggles is also very sobering and helps us to close any gaps between where we think we are in our purity and where we really are in our purity. Sometimes we are doing much better than we may be giving ourselves credit for and then other times we are doing much worse than we are telling ourselves we are doing. No matter which side of the spectrum you are on it is better to have a clear picture of where you really are than for you to be in the dark about where you stand.

I remember one time when I was a member of a health and fitness group in which I had to report to the coach of the program weekly. For weeks I consistently showed up and weighed the same amount. I had been working out regularly, but the weight would not come off. One day after completing my weigh-in I tried my best to convince the coach that the lack of weight loss made no sense because I had been doing everything right. I even explained that I wasn't eating much food at all. The coach looked at me and said with great conviction "There is no other explanation for you weighing as much as you do except you are eating too much!". I was so shocked at his audacity to suggest that I was eating too much food when I knew for sure that I was eating very few calories per day. The coach suggested that I start a food journal. I took the challenge with ease. The first day I started the journal I knew that the coach was right in his "accusation." I quickly realized that my calorie intake was the problem. I was consuming twice, if not three times, more calories per day than I thought I was consuming. I was so shocked to see the number of calories I was taking in daily all while thinking that I was doing pretty good in my eating. The journal showed me the true number of calories I was consuming. Once I saw the truth it was so much easier to develop an effective game plan that would get me to the next level in my weight-loss and fitness journey. Journaling daily will help you in the same way my food journal helped me with my weight loss. The journal will show you the truth about yourself and your struggles in purity. As I stated before you will need to be completely honest in your daily journal entries in order to fully experience the benefits of journaling.

How To Journal Effectively

It is easy for us to just go through the motions when it comes to spending time in God's word daily. Sometimes we find ourselves just reading in order to say that we have read our bibles. This can even happen when it comes to taking notes and making journal entries. We can get into the habit of just writing something down in order to complete the task of journaling. Other times we may be sincere in reading our bibles to genuinely hear what God is saying to us, but we schedule our study time poorly and don't give ourselves enough time to be still and meditate on what we are reading. Poor time planning can also hinder us from being able to really hear our own thoughts clearly before writing them down in our journals. For us to journal effectively we need to be intentional about our journal time. Praying for focus and praying to get what God wants us to get out of our time in his word before we start our daily meditation and journaling will help us to stay away from just going through the motions of reading and journaling. We also need to make sure that we are allowing ourselves an adequate amount of time to really be still and focus on the things we are reading and writing. We will need to carve out at least 30 minutes per day during which we will shut out everything else in the world so that we can hear from God and be genuine in our journaling. This scheduled time should be a protected time. We should guard this time like treasure. The time we spend connecting with God alone is the most important part of our days as it will set our hearts and minds on what God desires and prepare us for all the temptations we'll face throughout our day. Scheduling this time will be easy but sticking to meeting with God daily during this time will be hard as the enemy will use anything and everything to keep us from following through with this commitment. We will need to keep in mind that Satan does not want us to meet with God consistently in reading, prayer, and journaling because this is one of the most powerful weapons, we can use against him and his schemes.

Avoid the Temptation to Skip Journaling

As the temptations to skip come your way you will have to make up your mind to be committed no matter what. Staying committed to your meeting with God may even require you to change some things in your daily life. One thing you may need to change is when and how you go to bed. You must start going to bed earlier if it is a struggle for you to wake up early enough for you to spend at least 30 minutes meeting with God. If you have a lot of noise and distractions happening in your household in the morning, then you may have to plan to either get out of bed during a time at which everyone else is still sleeping or you may have to leave the house and go away or go outside to a solitary place so you can focus.

Mark 1:35-37 says," *Very early in the morning, while it was still dark, Jesus got up, left the house and went off to a solitary place, where he prayed. Simon and his companions went to look for him, and when they found him, they exclaimed: "Everyone is looking for you!".*

Mark writes about the fact that Jesus got up early in the morning while it was still dark. Jesus made sure that he met with God before he started his day. He also went off to a solitary place where he could be alone and away from distractions. These suggestions may seem radical but the reward of making these sacrifices will be worth it. You are reading this book because you have a desire to be closer to God and to live a purer life than you are currently living. The key to living a pure life is to live according to God's word. This book and the scriptures in it are designed to help you read and remember what God's word says about sexual purity. Spending time meeting with God while going through this book will help you to renew your mind about sexual purity so that you can be transformed (Romans 12:2).

Using Your Journal as A Tool

If you are anything like me, you have read books that included journals or notes sections, but you decided that reading the content was more important than using the journal pages in the book. I have done this many times when reading books in which a response section was provided. I am very guilty of doing this in my past. I've now come to understand that reading those books without taking time to write out my responses kept me from experiencing the full impact of the content in the book.

I implore you to make the most of this opportunity for spiritual growth and don't cheat yourself by downplaying the impact that journaling daily will have on your success in this detox. Your daily journal entries are going to be the tool that brings all parts of your detox together. Your journal will also be used to help guide you through your conversations with your detox partner or group.

Your journal will serve as a tool in your detox journey in many ways. Let us discuss the ways journaling can be a tool.

Writing Out Your Purity Goals

Purity goals for each person are just as different as purity struggles are for each person. As people we struggle with purity in many different ways. What one person needs to grow in may be something that the next person has never even struggled with. One person can be struggling with having lustful thoughts and in turn have the goal of learning how to take their thoughts captive and stop lusting. A different person may struggle with flirting and may have the goal of setting boundaries in how they talk to and interact with people. Writing out your purity goals helps you to make your purity journey personal instead of the journey being a big broad overwhelming and ambiguous goal of just being pure. I'm sure we have all had the feeling that becoming totally pure is like eating an elephant. Do we want to become totally pure, yes! Will it help if we focus on eating the elephant of becoming totally pure one bite at a time with true growth and repentance in each area, yes! The goal stays the same even if the plan of how to reach it changes. Writing out your specific purity goals and focusing on doing excellent in those goals will be the bites that eventually help you eat the elephant of sexual purity. Though we know that spiritual purity is all encompassing and not just isolated to the sexual aspect of our lives, the purity detox is designed to help us overcome our personal struggles in the area of sexual purity.

It is important to write out what your purity goals are weekly and read over them daily because as you meditate on the daily scripture readings the word of God will illuminate your life and bring to light more truth about what you need to change in order to reach those goals. Don't think you have to change your purity goals on a weekly basis just because you are writing them down weekly. If your goal stays the same, then you should write that same goal down weekly in response to the purity goal question in your journal. Even if the weekly goal never changes then writing it down weekly is still very helpful as it will help to ingrain this goal of purity in your mind and keep it in your heart.

Developing A Purity Vision

Your desire to please God is the most important desire and focus you have. I encourage you to take this journey to purity a step further by getting a vision for how the more spiritually mature version of yourself will look as you grow in your purity. Get a vision for how you will handle temptations. Get a vision for the person you will be as you set new boundaries in your life that keep you from giving in to Satan's schemes to get you into sexual sin. Get a vision for the person you will be when you can share with others about how God helped you overcome your struggles in sexual purity in order to help them. Create a specific vision for what your new life in sexual purity will look like.

Later in this book you will be able to bring together your purity vision by completing the purity vision journal entry. This will help you to get a clear picture of who you are aiming to become in your purity. We all know that it is God's will for us to live pure lives, but some of us are hoping to show up in better ways in specific parts of our lives. For example, you may be a married person who is seeking to be more trustworthy in your marriage by living in true sexual purity and integrity, you may be a single person who is desiring to have better boundaries in your dating experiences, or you could be wanting to experience the peace of being godly in the entertainment choices you make behind closed doors. Whether or not any of the examples I listed apply to you, it is important that you use the purity vision section of your journal to write out your own personal purity vision.

Having a vision for growth and victory in our sexual purity is key in helping us to both see our growth and be aware of our needs for growth. Writing out a vision in our purity will also help us to develop a plan for how to become the person we envision ourselves becoming.

Let's look at Habakkuk 2:2

"And the Lord answered me: "Write the vision; make it plain on tablets, so he may run who reads it." (ESV)

The above verse is part of a conversation that God was having with Habakkuk. God told him to write the vision down and make it plain for the purpose of whoever reads the vision may be able to run with the vision.

Though God was telling Habakkuk to write down a specific vision which God was giving to Habakkuk, the concept of writing down our visions so that we can run with them is still an applicable concept to our purity vision. We write to remember, and we need to be reminded so that we stay the course as we are tempted to shrink back into our old patterns, habits, and choices. Reading our purity vision daily even when we don't think it to be necessary will help us to stay focused on where we are determined to get to in our purity. We need to write the vision down and read it to ourselves daily so that we can continue to run with it.

Let us look at Proverbs 29:18

" Where there is no vision, the people perish: but he that keepeth the law, happy is he."

The verse listed above shows us another reason why it is important to have a vision. A lot of times we just have a general desire to live a life of sexual purity. Often, we don't have a targeted outcome in mind when we start talking about and studying sexual purity. If we're not careful we will be more focused on a shift in our feelings about sexual desire rather than a behavior changing paradigm shift. Waiting for our feelings to change towards sexual desire is like waiting to feel like working. We know that if we only work when we feel like working then we would have some serious financial problems. What drives us to work when we don't feel like working is the outcome of receiving the money, we need to pay our bills and save money. If we want to grow in sexual purity, we must get our minds to shift about why sexual purity is important. Proverbs 29:18 helps us to see that if we don't have vision we will perish. We need a vision for every aspect of our lives even in the area of purity. Shooting in the dark is not the way we will hit the mark of growing in purity. We can't just throw scripture at our lives hoping it will stick to something. We must be intentional in dealing with our own personal sin and struggles. As we write out our visions for where we want to be in our sexual purity, we will have an outcome in mind to help us navigate temptation and make the right choices when they are hard to make.

Processing God's Word

Another way that journaling will be a very helpful tool in this journey to purity is helping us to write out our thoughts about the scriptures in our daily reading. Reading God's word just to check it off the task list is not a good practice. God wants us to listen intently to what he says to us as we read His word. God wants us to process what the scriptures are saying and think about how they apply to our lives.

Let's look at what James 1:22 - 25 says...

"Do not merely listen to the word, and so deceive yourselves. Do what it says. Anyone who listens to the word but does not do what it says is like someone who looks at his face in a mirror and, after looking at himself, goes away and immediately forgets what he looks like. But whoever looks intently into the perfect law that gives freedom and continues in it—not forgetting what they have heard, but doing it—they will be blessed in what they do."

The verse above helps us to understand that our lives don't get blessed through us just merely reading over scripture, but instead our lives are blessed as we remember what God's word says and put it into practice.

In the scripture response section of your journal, you will take a few minutes to meditate on the daily scripture reading and then write out what you gathered from that scripture and write out how you plan to apply it to your life. This part of journaling is designed to help you do exactly what James 1:22 talks about, which is being a doer of the word and not just merely reading the word and forgetting what it says.

Taking Your Thoughts Captive

The most common way for Satan to get us into sexual sin is through our thoughts. Most forms of sexually acting out start with an impure or inappropriate thought that was not shut down at a thought level. The thought was tolerated and therefore became a full-on desire and was in turn put into action of some sort. By using the temptations section of your journal, you will not only be able to get the thoughts out on paper so you can see more clearly what is feeding your sexual struggles, but you will also be able to take these thoughts captive by writing them out and then you can write down what God's word says about the thought you are having. This may seem like a challenge but the fruit it will produce in your purity will be beyond worth it.

Let's look at what 2 Corinthians 10:4-5...

"The weapons we fight with are not the weapons of the world. On the contrary, they have divine power to demolish strongholds. We demolish arguments and every pretension that sets itself up against the knowledge of God, and we take captive every thought to make it obedient to Christ."

In the verse above we see that we have the power to demolish strongholds! I don't know about you, but I have experienced feeling as if Satan had a stronghold on me in my purity before. I have had to fight for my life to overcome some temptations and struggles in purity. 2nd Corinthians 10:4-5 shows us that we do not fight these battles with weapons of this world. We need spiritual weapons to win the fight for our purity. In Ephesians 6:17 the word of God is said to be "the sword of the spirit". By writing out scriptures that deal with the inappropriate thoughts you are having you are fighting with the most powerful weapon we have, the word of God!

This practice will help you to not only overcome the temptation you are having now, but it will also help you grow in being prepared to respond to Satan's temptations in general.

Let us look at Matthew 4:1-4

"Jesus was led by the Holy Spirit to a desert. There He was tempted by the devil. Jesus went without food for forty days and forty nights. After that He was hungry. The devil came tempting Him and said, "If You are the Son of God, tell these stones to be made into bread." But Jesus said, "It is written, 'Man is not to live on bread only. Man is to live by every word that God speaks.'"

In the verse above we see that Jesus himself fought off Satan's temptations by using God's word against the things Satan was saying to use to tempt Jesus. If we are going to imitate Christ, then we have the answer on how to overcome temptation as Christ did. We want the outcome Jesus had in defeating temptation so it only makes sense that we must use what Jesus used, which is God's word. If anyone was going to be able to overcome Satan's temptations without having to use God's word that person would be Jesus, but even being the perfect Son of God himself he still used God's word in the face of temptation. We are not stronger that Jesus and therefore we need to use God's word no less than Jesus needed to.

It is easy for us to just shrug a shoulder at temptation as if it will just "magically" go away if we blow it off but most of us know that at times when we don't stop and actually take our thoughts captive, we have found ourselves in some form of sin. We can't be lazy in how we deal with temptation if we want to be victorious in our purity. Writing down your thoughts in your journal and writing a scriptural response will help you to grow and mature in dealing with temptations.

Making Clear Confessions

I'm sure that I am not alone in the experience of knowing the bold confession I need to make to my spiritual partner about some sin I've committed and the difference in the way my confession sounds by the time I talk to my partner. On my way to talk with my partner I plan to sound like the tax collector in the parable about the tax collector and the pharisee, but I end up sounding more like the pharisee by the time my pride causes me to minimize my sin. Our human nature is to hide things we feel ashamed of. Writing full transparency confessions in our journals will help us to be able to use our journals to help us give our spiritual partners a full transparency confession by reading our journal entries to them.

Let us look at James 5:16...

"Tell your sins to each other. And pray for each other so you may be healed. The prayer from the heart of a man right with God has much power."

In the scripture above we see that we get healing/overcoming sin through openly telling each other about our sins. For this reason, you will need to find someone with whom you can openly tell your sin to.

In this chapter we have gone over some of the great ways to use our journals and the reasons why it is important for us to journal daily. Being consistent in answering the questions in your daily journal will help you to be successful in your detox.

Chapter Two

Confession

Coming Out of Darkness

"If we confess our sins, he is faithful and just and will forgive us our sins and purify us from all unrighteousness."

1 JOHN 1:9

The first thing I addressed in chapter one was the importance of daily journaling. Though journaling is paramount in this detox, confession is step one in starting the detox process. Confession is the first thing you want to do because we can't overcome hidden sin. There is a saying that I say, and I live by which is "hidden sin is the beginning of the end". Confession may seem optional, but the bible tells us that confession is key to forgiveness, healing, and coming close to Christ. It is God's design that whatever is done in the dark must come to the light.

God Has Seen It Already

Let's look at Hebrews 4:13...

"Nothing in all creation is hidden from God's sight. Everything is uncovered and laid bare before the eyes of him to whom we must give account."

In reading Hebrews 4:13 we see that God already knows everything we do. Nothing is hidden from God's sight. This may cause you to wonder why it is important to confess our sins to God and man if God has already seen everything we've done. Even though God has already seen our sins we still need to humble ourselves and confess our sins. When someone wrongs us, we already know they've done something wrong to us, but our desire is to see them acknowledge that they did us wrong and to take full responsibility for what they did.

Knowing that God has already seen our sin should help us to feel less pressure about confessing our sin to God and man. As Hebrews 4:13 says "everything is laid bare before the eyes to whom we must give account." We do not have to give account to man, but we must give account to God. God is the one whom we will have to answer to for every sin we commit and therefore He should be the only one whose judgment we are concerned about. Though the bible calls us to confess our sin to man we don't need to fear judgment of man. Our God has already seen our sin and He just wants us to humble ourselves, confess, and genuinely take responsibility for our sins so that he can gladly forgive us.

Everything Gets Exposed

Let us look at Luke 8:17...

"For nothing is hidden that will not be made manifest, nor is anything secret that will not be known and come to light."

The verse above shows us that it is inevitable that whatever is done in the dark will come to the light. It may seem that it is our decision as to whether we want to get open and bring our sins and struggles to light, but that is not true. The sin we commit in the dark eventually comes to the light either through our sin growing and being exposed through our behavior and decisions, through God just allowing us to be "caught in the act", or through our own confession of those sins. Whichever way sin gets exposed it is inevitable that it will come to light. God wants us to choose to humbly bring our sin to the light through confession to both God and man. We confess our sin to God to humble ourselves in his sight and we confess sin to man so that they can pray for us and partner with us in overcoming those sins. Both parts of confession are super important and key in us overcoming sin and moving into healing and repentance.

It is Best If We Just Confess

Let us look at Psalm 32:5 ...

"Then I acknowledged my sin to you
and did not cover up my iniquity.
I said, "I will confess
my transgressions to the Lord."
And you forgave
the guilt of my sin."

Let us also look at James 5:16 ...

"Therefore, confess your sins to each other and pray for each other so that you may be healed. The prayer of a righteous person is powerful and effective."

In Psalm 32:5 we see David's humble attitude towards God. David said he decided to confess his sin to God and not cover it up. We must be humble in our attitude about our sin if we want God to forgive us. God is ready to forgive us and embrace us, but God gives that grace to us when we are humble. It is prideful of us to act as if any sin we commit is no big deal. God desires for us to have a godly sorrow about any sin and part of that godly sorrow is confessing our sins. In this verse David said the Lord forgave David's sin. If we want forgiveness, then we must be willing to admit that we are wrong in the sight of God.

James 5:6 tells us that we need to confess our sins to each other and pray for each other. Confessing our sins to each other helps to bring sin out in the open and it frees us from guilt of hidden sin. I have not studied any science behind how hidden sin can affect our physical health, but I can imagine that guilt can create strain on our relationship with God, our relationships with other people and on our bodies. I once heard a story from a friend who is a psychologist about a man who was hiding things from his wife and lying to her about those things. My friend who is a psychologist said he had recommended that the man confess the things he was hiding to his wife. The man refused to tell his wife the truth and eventually he developed a severe pain in his back that seemed to have come out of nowhere. The man's doctors had tried treating his back with various therapies and treatments, but nothing would help. My friend, the psychologist, believed that the back pain was the man's hidden sin "crying out" in the man's body. I have no proof to support my friends' belief, but I do find it to be believable. Regardless of the effects hidden sin can have on our health, being open with other trustworthy people allows those people to join us in our battle against that sin by praying for us.

Confessing our sins to a person may be uncomfortable to some people but we see, in James 5:16, it is biblical.

We're Blessed When We Confess

Let us also look at 1 John 1:1-9...

"This is the message we have heard from him and declare to you: God is light; in him there is no darkness at all. If we claim to have fellowship with him and yet walk in the darkness, we lie and do not live out the truth. But if we walk in the light, as he is in

the light, we have fellowship with one another, and the blood of Jesus, his Son, purifies us from all sin.

If we claim to be without sin, we deceive ourselves and the truth is not in us. If we confess our sins, he is faithful and just and will forgive us our sins and purify us from all unrighteousness."

We receive so many wonderful things from just humbly confessing our sin. We get true fellowship with other believers when we confess our sin. There is a dividing wall between us and other people when we're living in darkness. It is no coincidence that we feel distant, awkward, and insecure around other believers when we are hiding sin.

We also see that we have the blessing of Jesus' blood purifying us when we confess our sin. If we received no other benefit from confessing our sin than Jesus' blood purifying us, then we would still be beyond blessed!

Confessing our sins not only frees us from the burden of guilt but it also brings us into a closeness with God and his people.

Now that we have established the importance of confessing our sins we now have to plan to confess our sexual sins to both God and man. Who is a person whom you feel comfortable being open about confidential matters with and who also is a believer? The person who comes to your mind might be the person you can get open and honest with about your sexual sin and struggles. You want to make sure you pick someone who loves God and who loves you. You also want to make sure you trust the person you chose to open up to. Once you've chosen the person you will partner with then you may want to explain to them that you are doing the sexual purity detox and help them understand the reasons you'll be open with them.

Before you go confess to the person you choose you need to confess your sins to God. In the journal section of this book there is a dedicated section for you to write out the things you need to confess. Writing down the things you need to confess might make it a little easier for you to be open and honest in your conversation with God and with the person you chose as your detox partner.

This step is key to being successful in your detox because you want to make sure you have a clear conscience and a clean slate before starting your journey to a new beginning in sexual purity. You want God to be able to lavish his grace on you and take you great places because you chose to humble yourself in his sight by confessing sins he has already seen.

Let us look at James 4:6 before moving on

*"And he gives grace generously. As the Scriptures say,
    "God opposes the proud
        but gives grace to the humble."*

Chapter Three
Freedom Through Fasting

"Fasting with a pure heart and motives,
I have discovered, brings personal revival, and adds power to our
prayers. Personal revival occurs because fasting is an act of humility. Fasting
gives opportunity for deeper humility as we recognize our sins, repent,
receive God's forgiveness, and experience His cleansing of our soul and
spirit. Fasting also demonstrates our love for God and our full confidence in
His faithfulness."

BILL BRIGHT

asting is at the heart of this detox. The flesh has a mind of its own and it must be brought into submission to God. Gaining more control over our flesh is part of why we will be fasting during this detox but the most important reason we will be fasting is to humble ourselves before God. God wants to be our strength, but we must humble ourselves for God to step in. As we read in the last chapter "God opposes the proud but gives grace to the humble". When we fast, we are saying to God "I need you!". The fasting part of this detox will last for the full 21 days of the detox. Fasting for 21 days may seem intimidating but it will be worth every minute of it. God responds to us fasting. This detox is for the purpose of getting closer to God and living the kind of life he called you to live. God will see your humility. There are some very important things to note about how we should fast, and we will study those things in this chapter. In the bible Jesus tells us that fasting is necessary in order to overcome some things. The bible also shows us that fasting is an important part of our walk with God.

Fixing Your Mind to Fast

There are a few different parts of fasting that you will need to establish before starting your fast. You will need to decide what you are fasting from, how long you will fast for, and what perimeters you will set in order to keep your fast. You want to make up your mind about how you will do your fast before you start fasting so that you can make sure you are fixed on your fast. In other words, you want to be committed to your fast.

. There are many diverse types of fasts according to the bible. In scripture there are times when people fasted from food and water entirely and there are times when people only abstained from certain foods. It is your decision as to what kind of fast you choose to do. You choose whether you want to fast from food entirely and drink only liquids, if you will do water only fast, or if you just want to abstain from certain foods during your fast. The goal with fasting is that it should be a sacrifice that is genuinely a sacrifice and at a heart level it should focus our hearts on God. I personally like to do a liquid only fast for this fast because it helps to focus my heart on God and it keeps me in a constant headspace of remembering what I'm sacrificing for.

Another part of fasting is setting a duration of time for which you will fast. In the bible Moses fasted for forty days and forty nights, Esther called a three day fast, David and his men fasted only until evening when Saul was killed, David also fasted for seven days as he pleaded with God for his child's life, Daniel fasted for 21 days, and Jesus fasted for forty days and forty nights. This detox is a 21-day detox. The idea is that you will fast for the entire 21 days of this detox. This is why it is important for you to really think through what you want to fast from during this fast before you start the fast. The decision is yours as far as how long you will fast. You can choose to fast all day for the twenty-one days, or you can choose to fast for half the day each day. I have done fasting during which I only fasted from 6 AM to 6 PM, or from 6 PM to 6 AM each day. You want to fix your mind to whatever amount of time you decide to spend fasting. It is important to God that when we make a vow or a commitment to him that we keep that commitment.

Let us look at Ecclesiastes 5:4-5 ...

"When you make a promise to God, don't delay in following through, for God takes no pleasure in fools. Keep all the promises you make to him. 5 It is better to say nothing than to make a promise and not keep it."

The scripture above shows us that we have to be careful when we make a vow to God and it's pleasing to God when we follow through and keep the vows we make to God.

For this reason, it is very important that we think through the details of our fast before we begin the fast and that we fix our minds on finishing the fast.

Fasting God's Way

It's not only important to God that we stick to the fasts, but it is important to God that we conduct ourselves the right way while fasting. God does not want us to be double minded in general as we live our lives, and God also wants us to conduct ourselves in a way that is right while we are fasting.

Let us look at Matthew 6:16-18 ...

"And when you fast, don't make it obvious, as the hypocrites do, for they try to look miserable and disheveled so people will admire them for their fasting. I tell you the truth, that is the only reward they will ever get. But when you fast, comb your hair and wash your face. Then no one will notice that you are fasting, except your Father, who knows what you do in private. And your Father, who sees everything, will reward you."

Let us also look at Isaiah 58:3-9...

'We have fasted before you!' they say.
'Why aren't you impressed?
We have been very hard on ourselves,
and you don't even notice it!'
"I will tell you why!" I respond.
"It's because you are fasting to please yourselves.
Even while you fast,
you keep oppressing your workers.
What good is fasting
when you keep on fighting and quarreling?
This kind of fasting
will never get you anywhere with me.
You humble yourselves
by going through the motions of penance,
bowing your heads
like reeds bending in the wind.
You dress in burlap
and cover yourselves with ashes.
Is this what you call fasting?
Do you really think this will please the Lord?
"No, this is the kind of fasting I want:
Free those who are wrongly imprisoned;
lighten the burden of those who work for you.
Let the oppressed go free,
and remove the chains that bind people.
Share your food with the hungry,
and give shelter to the homeless.
Give clothes to those who need them,
and do not hide from relatives who need your help.
"Then your salvation will come like the dawn,
and your wounds will quickly heal.
Your godliness will lead you forward,
and the glory of the Lord will protect you from behind.
Then when you call, the Lord will answer.

'Yes, I am here,' he will quickly reply."

Reading Matthew 6:16 -18 helps us to see that God does not want us to walk around announcing our fast in efforts to let other people know we are fasting. God does not want us to seek the applause and admiration of people. God wants our reward for fasting to be from him. We must seek only God's face alone when we are fasting. This scripture says that if we show off the fact that we are fasting then the reward of admiration from other people will be our only reward. In other words, our fast will be in vain if we do it to get approval and attention from people.

In Isaiah 58:3-9 God makes it very clear that there are fasts that God will not respond to at all. In this passage God called the Israelites out for the way they were living and behaving while they were fasting. God tells the Israelites that the kind of fasting they were doing will never get them anywhere and he explains that if they strive to live righteously during their fast then God will respond quickly to them.

Fasting is a spiritual act and practice. When we fast it puts us in a headspace in which we can see and hear God more clearly. There is an intimacy with God that comes through fasting the right way. God's word says that we should seek God with all our hearts. Fasting is part of seeking God and his will. During this detox you will be fasting and praying to overcome sexual sin. You will need to seek to hear what God wants to say to you to help you gain conviction and to renew your mind so you can be transformed in your purity. For God to respond to your fast you will have to fast in a way that is pleasing to him.

Fasting For Repentance and Restoration

Fasting is a way for us to humble ourselves before God. We know that Jesus has already died for the forgiveness of our sins, but that does not mean we get to continue in our sin. The response God desires for us to have to the cross is repentance. Jesus did his part and now it is up to us to do our part. If we're not careful we can live in a state of complacency that causes the cross to be one sided in our lives. When we live our lives to please ourselves and constantly ask God for forgiveness then we attempt to have a one-way relationship with Jesus. For us to experience true relationship with Jesus we have to respond to the cross with repentance.

Repentance is a decision that is followed by a process of changing. Sometimes we change in an instance, but then some sins are so insidious that we must pray and fast in order to overcome the behavior after we've made up our minds to repent. For example, even if we are able to instantly stop actively having sex with other people, the desire for sex may still cause us to struggle with lustful thoughts. Overcoming lust at a thought level can often be more challenging than quitting sexual activity. Sometimes repenting of lust can feel overwhelming because it's such a hidden and convenient sin to commit. Satan knows that lustful thoughts are an easier sin to get us to commit so he has "painted" the world from corner to corner with content that constantly tempts us with lust. Just because we are tempted does not mean we have to give in. God is able to strengthen us so we can resist the temptation to lust. As long as we genuinely commit our minds and hearts to striving for repentance God will help us overcome. The fact that you are reading this book says that you have already agreed with God that sexual purity is the goal. Deciding to humble ourselves in fasting is a powerful step in striving for repentance and growth.

Let us look at Luke 3:8 ...

"Produce fruit in keeping with repentance."

Let us look at Galatians 5:19-23 ...

"The acts of the flesh are obvious: sexual immorality, impurity and debauchery; idolatry and witchcraft; hatred, discord, jealousy, fits of rage, selfish ambition, dissensions, factions and envy; drunkenness, orgies, and the like. I warn you, as I did before, that those who live like this will not inherit the kingdom of God.

But the fruit of the Spirit is love, joy, peace, forbearance, kindness, goodness, faithfulness, gentleness and self-control. Against such things there is no law. "

Let us look at Ephesians 5:5 ...

"Be sure of this! No person who does sex sins or who is not pure will have any part in the holy nation of Christ and of God."

Let's look at Romans 12:2 ...

"Do not act like the sinful people of the world. Let God change your life. First of all, let Him give you a new mind. Then you will know what God wants you to do. And the things you do will be good and pleasing and perfect."

Luke 3:8 helps us to see that the way we produce spiritual fruit is by sticking with our decision to repent. To repent means to have a paradigm shift. We're looking at the dictionary meaning of the word paradigm which is "a standard, perspective, or set of ideas". A *paradigm* is a way of looking at something." If we have a paradigm shift then that means we will shift our standards, perspectives and ideas so that they are no longer in alignment with the world but instead they will be in alignment with God's word.

The passage in Galatians 5:19 - 23 explains that sexual immorality is an act that we commit when we are living according to our flesh. The passage also shows us that the opposite of living according to our flesh is to live according to the Holy Spirit. If we live according to the Holy Spirit then we will produce the fruits of the Spirit. One of the fruits listed in Galatians 5:23 is self-control. Self-control may seem like one of the hardest things to grow in when we are trying to muscle and white knuckle our way into being more self-controlled. Again, if we look at Luke 3:8 we see that God's word tells us that the way we produce fruit is by keeping with repentance. We have to keep fighting the good fight of repentance if we want to mature in having the fruit of the Holy Spirit. We won't be able to grow in the fruits of the spirit if we keep succumbing to the acts of the flesh. One way we can overcome being powerless to the flesh is by fasting and praying for Gods' strengthening.

Again, it's important that we understand that the first step in repentance is to go the right way in our thinking. As we see above in Romans 12:2 we can't continue to live like the world after we come into the Kingdom of God. We must decide to let God change our lives. Romans 12:2 also tells us to allow God to give us a new mind. In order for our lives to be changed we have to have a paradigm shift which is the meaning of repentance. Having a paradigm shift in our purity means to give up our old ways of thinking about how to handle sexual desires and take on God's way of thinking about how to handle those desires.

Amos 3:3 says, "Can two people walk together without agreeing on the direction?". This scripture in Amos 3:3 helps us to see that we have to be in agreement with someone in order to walk with them. How will we walk with God if we are still in agreement with the way the world thinks about how to handle our sexual desires? It's easy to say that we are "walking with God" and still holding on to the ways of this world. The only way we can truly walk with God is if we agree with Him and what his word says. It's not enough to agree that the word of God is true. We have to live in accordance with God's word in order to walk with God. Pride allows us to think we can have our cake and eat it too, spiritually speaking.

There are many false teachings in the world today which give believers the idea that we can live with one foot out in the world and the other foot in the Kingdom of God. One of these false teachings is the idea that we can live in sexual immorality and still go to Heaven. If we are truly striving to follow Jesus then we must pay close attention to what Jesus says. In Matthew 5:29-30 Jesus says, *"But I say to you that everyone who looks at a woman with lustful intent has already committed adultery with her in his heart. If your right eye causes you to sin, tear it out and throw it away. For it is better that you lose one of your members than that your whole body be thrown into hell. And if your right hand causes you to sin, cut it off and throw it away. For it is better that you lose one of your members than that your whole body go into hell."*

After reading this scripture in Matthew 5:29-30, let's ask ourselves this question; Why does Jesus suggest that the alternative to cutting off the thing that causes us to sin is our whole body being thrown into hell? Is Jesus suggesting that a lack of repentance can cause us to be thrown into hell? The point here is that if we are in sin then we need to do whatever it takes to stop sinning even if it's radical. We will touch on this verse more in chapter 9.

Ephesians 5:5 tells us that no person who sins sexually or is impure will have a part in the Holy nation of Christ. This scripture was written by Paul, and it was written after Christ has already died for our sins. How is it that we can be warned that our sin can lead to us not having a part in the Holy Nation of God after Christ has already died? Isn't the belief that after we come to Christ it is not possible for us to be treated according to our sin? Don't we believe that once we are saved there is no consequence for sin? Here in this scripture Paul, an apostle of Christ Jesus, warns us that if we keep committing sexual sin, then we will have no part in the Holy nation of God. We are called to be Holy so how do we reconcile living in sexual sin with being called to be holy. The motivation for repentance has to go beyond not wanting to sin and become a desire to live a holy life in the sight of God. Going from living in a world that is super-charged with sexual sin to living a life of striving for holiness can be very challenging, but with God all things are possible. We must thirst and hunger for righteousness (Matthew 5:6) both spiritually in our hearts and physically in terms of fasting. We have to want righteousness bad enough that we will do whatever wise and godly thing we can in order to have it. God is not looking for us to do extreme things just to convince him of our sincerity, but God is looking for hearts that are truly seeking to overcome sin.

Let us look at 1 Corinthians 7:10 - 11

"Godly sorrow brings repentance that leads to salvation and leaves no regret, but worldly sorrow brings death. See what this godly sorrow has produced in you: what earnestness, what eagerness to clear yourselves, what indignation, what alarm, what longing, what concern, what readiness to see justice done. At every point you have proved yourselves to be innocent in this matter."

The verse listed above gives us a clear picture of what godly sorrow looks like. Godly sorrow is eager to be right with God. Godly sorrow causes our hearts to be willing to do whatever it takes to repent. Can you honestly say that you have been willing to do anything to stop sinning sexually? Have you been willing to stop dating a person who is causing you to sin sexually? Have you been willing to stop listening to music that causes you to feel sexually aroused? What about not watching movies that open your heart to lust? There are so many more questions we could ask here but I think you get the picture. If you have not been willing to do anything it takes to repent of sexual sin, then you have not yet reached a heart of godly sorrow. I don't want you to count yourself out just because you don't already have godly sorrow. I want you to be sober and honest about where your heart has been so that you can move forward in the truth. David was sober and honest when he pleaded with God for a pure heart. David asked God to give him a pure heart and a contrite spirit in Psalms 51:10, "Create in me a pure heart, O God, and renew a steadfast spirit within me.". David wasn't caught up in the pride of refusing to admit that he had a heart issue.

As we journey through this detox and the fasting, we have to humbly accept and admit that we have a heart issue. Humbling ourselves before God in fasting invites God into our struggle and allows him to make us strong in our weaknesses. God wants to help us and create in us a broken and repentant heart.

Chapter Four

The Power of Prayer

---

*Therefore I tell you, whatever you ask in prayer, believe that you have
received it, and it will be yours*

Mark 11:24

I hope that by now you have gained an understanding of how necessary it is for us to strive wholeheartedly for sexual purity. We have discussed the importance of confession, and we've read what God's word says about how repentance is what God is calling us to. In the last chapter we discussed the way God wants us to conduct ourselves when we fast and how fasting will be a powerful part of this detox. Now let us take a look at another very powerful part of this detox which is prayer. Have you ever heard the saying "prayer changes things"? Prayer is the most powerful thing we can do in order to invite the power of God into our lives.

Let us look at Matthew 6:9-13...

"Pray then like this: "Our Father in heaven,
hallowed be your name.
Your kingdom come,
your will be done,
on earth as it is in heaven.
Give us this day our daily bread,
and forgive us our debts,
as we also have forgiven our debtors.
And lead us not into temptation,
but deliver us from evil. "

Let us look at James 5:16 again...

"Therefore confess your sins to each other and pray for each other so that you may be healed. The prayer of a righteous person is powerful and effective."

Let us also look at Ephesians 6:10-18...

"Finally, be strong in the Lord and in his mighty power. Put on the full armor of God, so that you can take your stand against the devil's schemes. For our struggle is not against flesh and blood, but against the rulers, against the authorities, against the powers of this dark world and against the spiritual forces of evil in the heavenly realms. Therefore put on the full armor of God, so that when the day of evil comes, you may be able to stand your ground, and after you have done everything, to stand. Stand firm then, with the belt of truth buckled around your waist, with the breastplate of righteousness in place, and with your feet fitted with the readiness that comes from the gospel of peace. In

addition to all this, take up the shield of faith, with which you can extinguish all the flaming arrows of the evil one. Take the helmet of salvation and the sword of the Spirit, which is the word of God.

And pray in the Spirit on all occasions with all kinds of prayers and requests. With this in mind, be alert and always keep on praying for all the Lord's people."

Lastly, let's take a look at Matthew 6:41...

" Watch and pray that you may not enter into temptation. The spirit indeed is willing, but the flesh is weak."

After reading Matthew 6:9-13 we know that Jesus himself tells us to pray for God to lead us away from temptation. Jesus was saying this to his disciples after they had asked him how they should pray. If you are not familiar with this conversation between Jesus and his disciples, then please go back and read the full chapter of Matthew 6. A very interesting thing for us to meditate on and note is the fact that Jesus uses the words "give us this day", referring to "today", in this passage of scripture. The reason it is interesting that Jesus uses the words "this day" as a part of his instructions for how they should pray is because it is indicative that Jesus was teaching his disciples to cover themselves in this type of praying on a daily basis. Jesus could have said to his disciples "you shall never be tempted again" and granted them exemption from temptation if that were God's will. God allows us to have free will and in having free will we don't get exemption from temptation. It is the very nature of God that allows the whole buffet of sin to be placed right in front of us for our choosing. It is not God's will that we should choose to sin, but it is God's nature to not remove the possibility for us to do so. Jesus teaches us how to humbly come to God and ask that God lead us away from the temptations we face daily. Every day we get the freedom of making the choice to either give in to temptation or to ask God to strengthen us so that we will not succumb to it. Pride is what convinces us that we can do it on our own without asking for the help of God through prayer. Every day that we choose to skip the opportunity to invite the strength and power of God into our lives through praying like Jesus told us to, we are walking in pride and asking for trouble. It is a blessing that we have a God to whom we can go to daily and ask that he strengthen us against temptation, and he will do it.

In chapter two we looked at James 5:16 for an understanding of why we need to confess our sins to each other. Now in this chapter we want to pay attention to another very important part of this scripture. This verse tells us to pray for each other so that we may be healed. Some scholars teach that this verse is referring to healing of physical illnesses. The part we want to take away from this verse is in verse 16 which says the prayers of a righteous man are powerful and effective. In this scripture we are called to pray for each other. Whether we are praying for physical healing or for spiritual deliverance we are still able to pray for each other and our prayers for one another are powerful and effective.

Ephesians 6:10 - 18 is a very powerful and eye-opening passage. This passage clues us in on the very fact that we are not fighting against things that are in the physical realm, but instead we are fighting against spiritual forces of evil. Even you, yes even you are not wrestling with the flesh itself. You are fighting a spiritual fight. The fact that we are fighting a spiritual fight should help us realize that we need spiritual weapons to win the fight. In this passage Paul gives us a list of the things we need in order to stand against the devil's schemes. In verse 18 Paul ends the list with an "And" which is followed by his instruction to "pray in the Spirit on all occasions". We often read verses 14 - 17 as the list of armor gear, but if we pay attention to all what Paul is saying he does not move on from verse 14 - 17 to a new subject; no Paul continues the list by saying "and pray…". Verse 18 should bring us into the light of knowing that prayer is a very important part of fighting spiritually. When we are trying to overcome sexual sin in our lives, we must know we are not fighting a battle against our flesh. There is no physical remedy for overcoming sexual sin. The only way to overcome sexual sin is by using spiritual weapons. One of those key weapons that we must use is prayer.

Again, in Matthew 6:41 we see Jesus teaching his disciples how prayer shields from temptation. Jesus tells his disciples to *"watch and pray that you may not enter into temptation."* We often just go about our days without praying for God to protect us from temptation and then we wonder why we are constantly succumbing to sin and temptation. If you have been struggling with sin and feeling powerless to the temptation of sexual sin, please pause for a minute and ask yourself if you have been praying daily for God's protection against temptation. If you have not been praying daily, I encourage you to get excited and look forward to how starting to pray every day for God to strengthen you against temptation is going to invite God's power in so you have finally have victory!

If we want to start to be victorious in the face of temptation, then we must pray daily as Jesus instructs in Matthew 6:9 - 13. We need to also allow others to pray for us after we have confessed our sin to them as we see in James 5:16. It is super important that we understand that prayer is part of how we arm ourselves in order to stand against Satan. Last but most definitely not least we have to understand that if Jesus' disciples were right there with Jesus in Matthew 26:41 and yet he still told them they need to watch and pray to keep from going into temptation, then how much more should we pray for God to keep us from giving into temptation.

During this detox it is imperative that you pray daily for God to strengthen you in your purity. I implore you to set a goal of spending at least thirty minutes each day in prayer. Asking God for his help daily will inevitably help to change your life.

Chapter Five
Preparation Through

Meditation

How can a young man keep his way pure?
By guarding it according to your word.

Psalms 119:9

This chapter excites me personally. There is nothing more exciting to talk about than the word of God. Yes, we've discussed the word of God throughout this entire book so far but in this chapter, we get to look at what the word of God says about reading the word of God. Looking at what God's word says about itself is so exciting to me! Of course, reading the word is not enough, the more important thing is to put the word into practice. Knowing Gods' word is the first step to obeying his word. As we study and meditate on God's word daily it will get deposited into our memories making it easier for us to recall as we face situations and temptations throughout our day. Once we have scriptures memorized, they become a part of our arsenal against Satan. The bible calls scripture the "sword of the spirit". Who wants to show up to a knife fight with a butter knife? I'd much rather show up with a sword! As we go through this journey to maturing in sexual purity then we need to begin the practice of meditating on the word of God daily so that we can be prepared to face the temptations of the enemy.

Let us look at Psalms 119:9-11...

"How can a young man keep his way pure?
By guarding it according to your word.
With my whole heart I seek you;
let me not wander from your commandments!
I have stored up your word in my heart,
that I might not sin against you."

Before we move forward with a deeper look at what God's word says about meditating on scripture, I feel we must pause here and meditate on what this verse in Psalms 119:9-11 tells us. The question the psalmist raised was "how does a young man keep his way pure?". He followed that question with the answer which is "by guarding it according to your word". This is a key thing for us to note and understand. Purity is freedom from immorality. If we want to have lives that are free of immorality, then we must understand that God's word is provided to us for that very reason. The word of God is a guide for coming out of immorality and coming into holiness. The psalmist knew exactly what he needed to do in order to keep his life pure. In verse 10 here he explains that he seeks God with his whole heart, and he desires to never stray from Gods' commandments. This is the kind of heart God desires for us to have. We live in a world that is so full of worldly views and opinions and that makes it even easier today to stray from the commandments of God. Our need for daily meditation on Gods' word is greater than ever before, yet Christians often treat reading the word of God daily as optional. Verse 11 really brings it all home by the psalmist explaining that he stores the word of God up in his heart so that he may not sin against God. Can you imagine how much stronger your ability to resist sexual sin would be if you truly took time to meditate on God's word daily in a way that allows you to "store it in your heart" and commit it to your memory. During this detox we will be learning how to meditate on Gods' word in a way that helps us to really take it into our hearts and minds and not just glaze over it to get it off the "good Christian checklist". We want the powerful word of God to live in us in a way that makes it useful and effective in keeping our way pure.

Let us look at Psalms 1:1-3...

"Blessed is the one
   who does not walk in step with the wicked
or stand in the way that sinners take
   or sit in the company of mockers,
but whose delight is in the law of the Lord,
   and who meditates on his law day and night.
That person is like a tree planted by streams of water,
   which yields its fruit in season
and whose leaf does not wither—
   whatever they do prospers."

This verse in Psalms 1:1-3 is so amazing! Let's stop here and meditate on what it says. Please take a moment and read through the above passage again slowly taking in each verse. If we look at verse one carefully, we must take note of the fact that it tells us we are blessed if we "do not" walk in step with the wicked. Can you imagine yourself walking along with people who are promoting sexual sin and who have no desire to change their minds about the fact that sexual sin is wrong. Imagine yourself walking with them. You, Gods' chosen child, are walking in a group of people who have chosen immorality as their way of life. Now imagine as you are walking with those people, and you hear God say these words to you "blessed is the one who does not walk in step with the wicked". How do you imagine yourself responding to God in that moment? I can't speak for you, but I imagine myself stopping in my tracks and turning to get out of that crowd as quickly as possible. The truth is, if we are not consistent spiritually, we can become so desensitized to sexual impropriety and indecency that we start to walk in step with the world. I encourage you to take a moment and take note of what ways you have started to walk in step with the world.

This verse also brings us back to the importance of meditating on Gods' word. Here the psalmist says he meditates on God's word day and night. Imagine how fortified your life would be spiritually if you took time to not just glance at a few verses in the morning but instead you paused and meditated on the word of God day and night. Ask yourself if you have been practicing meditating on Gods' word or if you have just been having some spiritual "fast food" daily. Maybe you have not been reading your bible much at all. No matter where you have been in terms of your bible study you can now get excited about where this detox journey is going to take you. During this detox you will practice meditating on Gods' word daily. You will have the meditation scriptures as part of your daily journaling. I encourage you to take five minutes at night to read your meditation scriptures again.

Verse 3 of Psalms 1 paints the picture of what the life of a person who meditates on the word of God day and night looks like. The Psalmist wrote, *"That person is like a tree planted by streams of water, which yields its fruit in season and whose leaf does not wither, whatever they do prosper."* Is the life listed in verse 3 the kind of life you want to live? In chapter 3 we looked at some scriptures about producing spiritual fruit. Here in verse 3 we know the psalmist is speaking of producing spiritual fruit because reading Gods' word is not quite the way to grow actual apples and oranges. In other words, we know this verse is not talking about edible fruit. When we look back at Galatians 5:22-23 we see what the fruits of the spirit are. Verse 3 also helps us to make the connection that meditating on Gods' word day and night helps us to produce the fruit Paul speaks of in Galatians 5:22 -23. The fruit we are particularly seeking to produce more of through this detox is the spiritual fruit of self-control. This verse also mentions that whatever a person who meditates on Gods' word day and night does prosper. God is letting us know that he blesses us when we sincerely seek him wholeheartedly. If God will bless us with prosperity in turn of us seeking him wholeheartedly, how much more will he bless us with victory in our sexual purity?

Let us look at Joshua 1:8...

"Keep this Book of the Law always on your lips; meditate on it day and night, so that you may be careful to do everything written in it. Then you will be prosperous and successful."

God told Joshua to meditate on Gods' word day and night so that he will be careful to do everything written in Gods' word. Meditating on Gods' word helps us to be able to use the word of God the way God wants us to. If we are not careful, we will become spiritually malnourished and too weak to really fight spiritually when faced with temptation. Carving out time to sit and meditate on God's word daily is an absolute must if we really want to mature in sexual purity. This is not to suggest that merely reading the bible will change us. The truth is that it is easy to read the bible and still live in sin. Meditating on Gods' word is aimed at keeping Gods' word on our minds all day. In order for the word to be on our hearts all day we have to read it each day.

Satan would love for us to miss out on meditating because it is to his disadvantage when we know the bible and we're equipped to do what the word of God says. As you journey through this detox be alert of the enemy who wants to distract you from reading Gods' word so that you will be easier to manipulate into sin.

Let us look at 1 Peter 5:8...

"Keep awake! Watch at all times. The devil is working against you. He is walking around like a hungry lion with his mouth open. He is looking for someone to eat.".

Let us also look at Proverbs 3:1

"My son, do not forget my teaching. Let your heart keep my words. For they will add to you many days and years of life and peace."

Chapter Six

Starting The Detox

"... let us throw off everything that hinders and the sin that so easily entangles. And let us run with perseverance the race marked out for us,"

Hebrews 12:1

I want to personally encourage you about the fact that you have decided to do this detox. You made a great decision! This detox is not about just completing a program that will lead you to sexual purity. The purpose of this detox is to help you let go of spiritual toxins that are keeping you from the purity God has called you to. God calls us to come away from the ways of this world and to be set apart for him. The desire of God's heart is to have a holy people whom he can have to himself without sharing us with the world. In this detox you will learn how to equip yourself with the tools and weapons necessary for you to overcome sexual sin.

The previous chapters laid the foundation of this detox. The things we are going to discuss in this chapter are extremely important to you being successful in completing this detox.

The Most Important Steps

As we went over in chapter one in this detox you will need to commit to journaling daily and answering every question in your journal entries. As we established in chapter one of this book, journaling daily is going to help you to get the most out of this detox.

I hope you are ready and prepared for the daily practices of praying, meditating on God's word, confessing your sin and temptations, and fasting. More importantly, I hope you are ready for the refreshment and growth that will come with practicing these disciplines!

You will also need to pick a person to be your detox partner. Proverbs 27:17 says, *"As iron sharpens iron, so one person sharpens another."*
Having a trustworthy person to help you through this detox will help you to become sharper spiritually in the area of sexual purity. If you really want to grow during this detox you will have to humble yourself and allow your detox partner to be honest with you about the things you share with them. It will be helpful to your relationship with your detox partner if you openly invite them to be honest with you and to share scripture with you as you share with them about your journey. Ephesians 4:15 tells us *"... speaking the truth in love, we will grow to become in every respect the mature body of him who is the head, that is, Christ."*

This scripture makes it clear that a vital part of us maturing spiritually is by us speaking the truth to each other. Picking your detox partner is the first thing you will need to do before starting your 21-day detox journey. Make sure the person you pick to be your partner can commit to you. They will need to make themselves available to you for at least 20 minutes per day as you go over your journal entries with them. Throughout this detox you will be confessing your sins and temptations to your detox partner. The journal entry about confession is not in your daily journal to suggest that you will have something to confess daily. The confession section is in your journal so that you can be aware of where you are in your purity and so you can get help as you share with your detox partner. You will also want to spend time praying with your detox partner.

Another great way to do the detox is by starting a detox group at your local ministry or by inviting your friends to do the detox with you. Doing this detox as a group will only be helpful if you do it with people who are like minded and who believe in living a life of sexual purity. If you chose to do this detox as a group, then you all will need to agree on how everyone in the group will have their own individual detox partner. You will need to set rules and boundaries for keeping the things that are shared by each group member confidential. Having one group meeting per week for the three weeks of the detox may help your group as well. The individual partners or pairs will need to commit to a time at which they can speak with each other daily.

Stepping Away from The Noise

If you want to make the very most of this detox it's going to be good for you to take a break from social media. One of the main goals of this detox is to remove spiritual toxins from our lives, both internal toxins such as impure thinking and even external toxins such as impure entertainment and company. I implore you to turn off all worldly television shows, music, podcast, and YouTube videos. I encourage you to only watch content that is Christian/spiritual content during this detox. Listening to only Christian and gospel music during this 21 day detox period will help you to focus more on God and help to detox your mind from worldly influences. You will be the one to decide how you go about doing this detox, but I assure you that if you give up all worldly entertainment and only watch and listen to Christian content then you will be greatly refreshed spiritually in turn.

By now I am sure you are all set and ready to complete these 21 days of The Sexual Purity Detox. I am so excited for you! I have already been praying for you that you will be refreshed in your purity and your walk with God in greater ways than you can ask think or imagine. If this detox does for you what it has done for me you are embarking on becoming a whole new person in your sexual purity! To God be all glory!

Write The Vision and Make It Plain

Before you start your purity detox journey it is important for you to write the vision you have for where you want this journey to lead you. On the following page you will find your vision statement journal entry. Now it's time to write your vision statement!

Purity Vision

1. List two words that you would like to describe you in the area of sexual purity (e.g., integrity, godly)

____

____

2. List something you want people/a person whom you have relationship(s) with to be confident about when it comes to your purity.

____

____

3. List something you want God to be pleased with you about when it comes to your purity.

____

____

Purity Vision

4. Combine all three of your answers to questions 1 - 3 into one single statement.

Example Given

If you answered 1. godly, 2. spouse can be confident that I won't view inappropriate content, 3. God can trust me to not look at other people lustfully.

Then your vison statement might look like the following:

"My personal purity vision is to be a godly person whom my spouse can trust to not view inappropriate content and whom God can trust to guard my eyes from looking lustfully at other people.

Your Purity Vision

____

____

____

____

____

Chapter Seven
Detoxing The Heart

"Come near to God and he will come near to you. Wash your hands, you sinners, and purify your hearts, you double-minded."

James 4:8

In this first week of the detox we are meditating on what God's word says about sexual sin and the heart. The opening scripture for this chapter calls us to purify our hearts.

As we journal this week we will focus on purifying and protecting our hearts when it comes to sexual purity. The bible helps us understand that seeking to have a pure heart is our responsibility not Gods'. God will help us to change our hearts, but we get that help from God through humbly asking God for help. God is always here to help us as we reach for him, but we have to take the first step.

Cutting Out Contaminants

God calls us to be set apart from the world. This calling is one of the hardest things for some of us to accept. We live in a world that is very good at making sin and spiritual pollution look good and enticing. If we're not careful we'll find ourselves justifying indulging in entertainment and activities that cause us to stumble in our sexual purity. The enemy will try to even convince us that the very things that are triggering us to sin are not even capable of causing us to stumble. This is not a new scheme. The enemy has been using the tactic of minimizing and trivializing the impact of wrong choices since Eve in the garden. The common lie that we buy into is "this won't surely cause you to stumble" just as the enemy convinced Eve "you won't surely die." As part of this week's journaling, we'll be examining our lives to identify the things we need to cut out of our lives so that we can decrease temptation and gain victory in being sexually pure.

Let us look at Matthew 5:30...

"And if your right hand causes you to stumble, cut it off and throw it away. It is better for you to lose one part of your body than for your whole body to go into hell."

Matthew 5:30 tells us that it is better for us to cut off things that cause us to sin than for us to go to hell. We should note that this is Jesus, the savior of the world, himself saying to his disciples that we need to do whatever it takes to keep from going to hell. Let us notice that Jesus did not tell them to just come to him after they sin in order to keep from going to hell. No, he let them know that their repentance is part of them not going to hell.

The idea that we must repent is hard for some people to accept because we live in a world that hides the message of repentance while highlighting the message of grace.

Grace is to be used for the purpose of repenting. It is by grace that you can read this this book, making this decision to repent and seeking to grow in sexual purity. Grace is what allows us the opportunity to repent. Grace is an underserved chance to get it right. Repentance is the spiritual state we must be in to be right with God.

Jesus tells his disciples, "It is better for you to lose one part of your body than for your whole body to go into hell.". An important part of this week's detox will be getting honest about anything and anyone that is causing you to stumble and sin sexually. Once you identify what things must be cut off then you must ask yourself is it more important for you to keep these things in your life than it is for you to have victory in sexual purity.

It will benefit you to openly discuss the things you will need to change or cut off with your detox partner or your detox group so they can help you stay strong in your decision.

Setting Protective Boundaries

It is not only important for us to remove sources of temptation from our lives. It is equally important for us to set up boundaries in our lives that keep those temptations out. The example that comes to mind is if you are in a sexually immoral relationship and you now decide to repent of having sex in that relationship, the next step would need to be setting up boundaries that keep the two of you out of situations that can lead to having sex. One of those boundaries would be not being inside of each other's homes alone. Now you can take that same idea and apply it to any area of your life in which you will cut off things that tempt you sexually. If you have struggled with watching worldly shows that are filled with sex scenes, then maybe your boundary should be canceling the channel or app membership on which you watch that show. Another example is if talking on the phone with the opposite sex late at night causes you to feel tempted sexually then maybe you only talk on the phone with the opposite sex during the day and for a limited amount of time. If you have a situation with a co-worker whom you find very attractive and tempted by then maybe you will need to limit all of your interactions with them to being strictly business. Setting boundaries may not feel good but it is good. Everything needs boundaries. We enjoy the beauty of the ocean but if God had not set boundaries in place around it then it would not be very enjoyable. We also really enjoy the sun but if it were not held at a certain distance from the earth then it would destroy us. The same is true about sex. Sex is a very good thing, but God designed us to only truly and peacefully enjoy sex when we have it within the boundaries of marriage. As Christians, we are not anti-sexual in our beliefs, but we are anti-sexual immorality. Sex is only supposed to be had within the boundaries of marriage.

Let us look at Ephesians 5:3...

"But among you there must not be even a hint of sexual immorality, or of any kind of impurity, or of greed, because these are improper for God's holy people."

This verse in Ephesians 5:3 is showing us that God not only wants us to not actually have sexual intercourse outside of marriage, but God calls us to not even let a little sexual sin in. We are to not even allow a hint. In other words, we can't even flirt with sexual sin. We live in a day and time when Christians who are abstaining from sex have watered down the call to purity by considering it pure to still perform oral sex and have it performed on themselves, engage in inappropriate touching, indulge in self-sex, watching other people have sex, acting out foreplay, and participating in many other impure acts. The verse we just read in Ephesians 5 leaves no room for confusion. The call is to not even let there be a hint. If we are to avoid even a hint, then that means we will need to set some serious boundaries in place to help us stay pure.

Let us look at 1 Corinthians 15:33...

"Do not be deceived: "Bad company ruins good morals."

Reading 1 Corinthians 15:33 opens our eyes to the fact that God wants us to be selective and wise about the company we keep. This does not mean that we mistreat people who don't live according to Gods' word, but it does mean for us to set boundaries on how much time we spend with them and what kind of involvement we have with them. If a person is trying to talk us into sinning sexually or even just speaking in sinful ways about sex, then we need to prevent them from having conversations with us about sex. In some cases, if a person refuses to respect our standards for purity, then we need to not keep their company at all.

Let us look at Genesis 2:16-17...

"And the Lord God commanded the man, "You are free to eat from any tree in the garden; but you must not eat from the tree of the knowledge of good and evil, for when you eat from it you will certainly die."

Most of us are familiar with this story in Genesis 2:26 - 17 and how God tells Adam he can eat freely of any tree in the garden but forbids Adam to eat of the one tree. This is God setting a boundary with Adam. God told Adam what he could do and what he could not do. We must be able to set these kinds of boundaries in our own lives. God was setting a protective boundary with Adam. The alternative to Adam not staying within the boundaries God set was to sin and to die as a result of his sin. Our boundaries need to be protective boundaries which we take as seriously as the boundary that God set with Adam instead of casually crossing the boundaries which we set for ourselves in the name of grace.

Cutting off the things which are contaminating our hearts with impurity and setting boundaries that mitigate the opportunities to sin sexually are going to be vital in detoxing our hearts.

Let us Start Week 1!

I am so excited for you and what God is going to do in you as you go through this detox!

As you meditate on each scripture for the days of this detox, I encourage you to take your bible study further by reading the full chapter in which each verse is found. This will help you to gain greater understanding of each verse. I also encourage you to read the meditation verse over again as you turn the pages of your journal. This will help you to commit the scriptures to memory. You may also want to write the verses down on index cards and take them with you so that you can read them throughout your day. The word of God is our sword, and we need it in order to fight the temptations of the enemy.

I hope that going through these first seven days of the detox helps you to treat your heart as though it is precious in God's sight and to protect the purity of it at all costs. May this week's studies strengthen you to be more victorious in sexual purity!

Let me pray for your week!

Heavenly Father, I come to you in Jesus' name thanking you that you have given us everything we need for life and godliness. I thank you that you don't call us to what is impossible but instead you call us to what is possible through you. I thank you for allowing the person reading this book the chance to repent and to come closer to you. I pray that you will deliver them from every stronghold that is on them in the area of sexual sin. I pray that as they read your word, they will be set free from worldly ways of thinking and be transformed by renewing their minds. I pray that they will be strengthened in their innermost being so that when the enemy comes after them with temptation they can say "no". I pray for them to gain a deep conviction to flee from sexual immorality. Please help them to resist the devil and draw near to you so that you can draw near to them. I pray that they will become victorious in purity and enjoy the beauty and freedom of walking with you in purity. I pray that they will be consistent in journaling daily during this first week of their detox and they reap amazing growth in turn. In Jesus name!

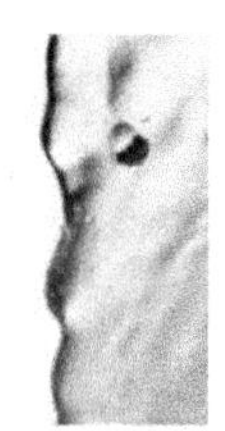

Week 1 Purity Goals

What is something you want to avoid doing for this entire week? (e.g., entertaining impure thoughts)

____

____

What scripture are you going to use to help fight the temptation to do the thing(s) you listed above?

____

____

At the end of this week come back here and tell how you did in reaching this goal this week.

____

____

Detox Day 1   Date:

Meditation Scripture:

*Psalm 51:10 "Create in me a pure heart, O God,
and renew a steadfast spirit within me."*

What failures do you need to confess today?

____

____

____

What temptations are you facing and praying about today?

____

____

____

____

____

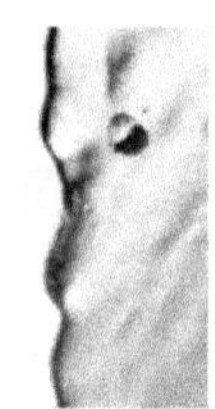

Detox Day 1   Date:

Meditation Scripture:

*Psalm 51:10 "Create in me a pure heart, O God,
and renew a steadfast spirit within me."*

How do you feel about the conversation you had
with your detox partner/group today?

____

____

____

Take time to write out your thoughts and prayers to
God about your purity.

____

____

____

____

I want to encourage you that you made an amazing
and godly decision to persevere in your purity today
Keep striving for godliness. God will strengthen you!
Keep Going!

Detox Day 2   Date:

Meditation Scripture:

Matthew 5:27-28 "You have heard that it was said, 'You shall not commit adultery'; but I say to you that everyone who looks at a woman with lust for her has already committed adultery with her in his heart.

What does this scripture show you about yourself?

____
____
____
____
____
____
____

How will you apply this scripture to your life?

____
____
____
____

  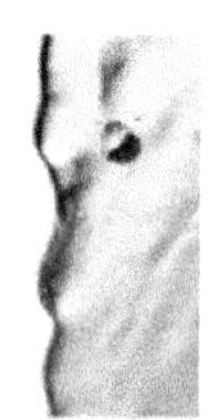

Detox Day 2   Date:

Meditation Scripture:

Matthew 5:27-28 "You have heard that it was said, 'You shall not commit adultery'; but I say to you that everyone who looks at a woman with lust for her has already committed adultery with her in his heart.

What boundaries do you need to set to help your heart become pure?

____

____

What entertainment do you need to give up to help your heart be pure?

____

____

What victories have you had in your purity today?

____

____

____

Detox Day 2   Date:

Meditation Scripture:

Matthew 5:27-28 "You have heard that it was said, 'You shall not commit adultery'; but I say to you that everyone who looks at a woman with lust for her has already committed adultery with her in his heart.

What failures do you need to confess today?

What temptations are you facing and praying about today?

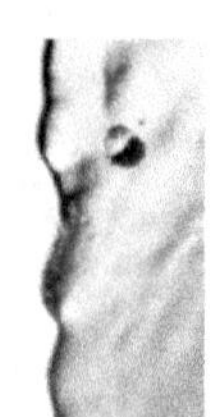

Detox Day 2   Date:

Meditation Scripture:

Matthew 5:27-28 "You have heard that it was said, 'You shall not commit adultery'; but I say to you that everyone who looks at a woman with lust for her has already committed adultery with her in his heart.

How do you feel about the conversation you had
with your detox partner/group today?

____
____

____

Take time to write out your thoughts and prayers to
God about your purity.

____
____
____
____

I want to encourage you that you made an amazing
and godly decision to persevere in your purity today
Keep striving for godliness. God will strengthen you!
Keep Going!

Detox Day 3

Date:

Meditation Scripture:

1 Thessalonians 4:3 "For this is the will of God, your sanctification; that is, that you abstain from sexual immorality;"

What does this scripture show you about yourself?

How will you apply this scripture to your life?

Detox Day 3

Date:

Meditation Scripture:

1 Thessalonians 4:3 "For this is the will of God, your sanctification; that is, that you abstain from sexual immorality;"

What boundaries do you need to set to help your heart become pure?

____

____

What entertainment do you need to give up to help your heart be pure?

____

____

What victories have you had in your purity today?

____

____

____

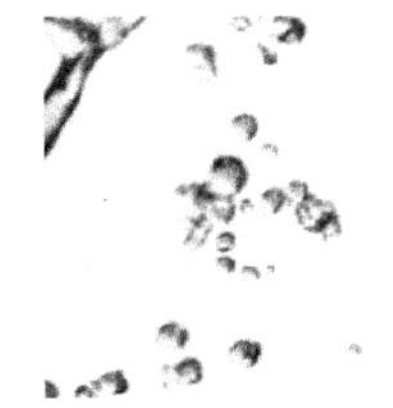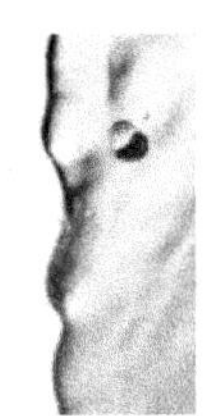

Detox Day 3

Date:

Meditation Scripture:

1 Thessalonians 4:3 "For this is the will of God, your sanctification; that is, that you abstain from sexual immorality;"

What failures do you need to confess today?

What temptations are you facing and praying about today?

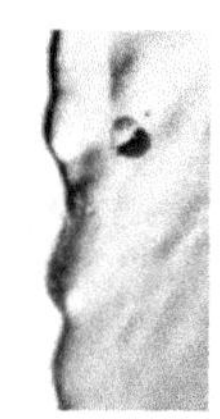

Detox Day 3   Date:

Meditation Scripture:

1 Thessalonians 4:3 "For this is the will of God, your sanctification; that is, that you abstain from sexual immorality;"

How do you feel about the conversation you had with your detox partner/group today?

____

____

____

Take time to write out your thoughts and prayers to God about your purity.

____

____

____

____

I want to encourage you that you made an amazing and godly decision to persevere in your purity today Keep striving for godliness. God will strengthen you!
Keep Going!

Detox Day 4

Date:

Meditation Scripture:

Mark 7:21 "For it is from within, out of a person's heart, that evil thoughts come—sexual immorality, theft, murder,"

What does this scripture show you about yourself?

How will you apply this scripture to your life?

Detox Day 4   Date:

Meditation Scripture:

Mark 7:21 "For it is from within, out of a person's heart, that evil thoughts come—sexual immorality, theft, murder,"

What boundaries do you need to set to help your heart become pure?

What entertainment do you need to give up to help your heart be pure?

What victories have you had in your purity today?

  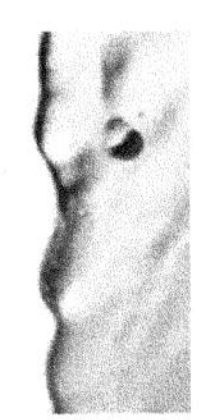

Detox Day 4   Date:

Meditation Scripture:

Mark 7:21 "For it is from within, out of a person's heart, that evil thoughts come—sexual immorality, theft, murder,"

What failures do you need to confess today?

____

____

What temptations are you facing and praying about today?

____

____

____

____

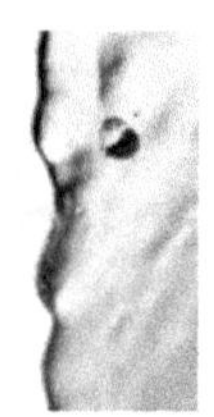

Detox Day 4

Date:

Meditation Scripture:

Mark 7:21 "For it is from within, out of a person's heart, that evil thoughts come—sexual immorality, theft, murder,"

How do you feel about the conversation you had
with your detox partner/group today?

____

____

____

Take time to write out your thoughts and prayers to
God about your purity.

____

____

____

____

I want to encourage you that you made an amazing
and godly decision to persevere in your purity today
Keep striving for godliness. God will strengthen you!
Keep Going!

  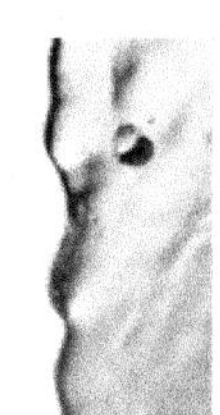

Detox Day 5

Date:

Meditation Scripture:

*Proverbs 4:23 "Above all else, guard your heart,
for everything you do flows from it."*

What does this scripture show you about yourself?

How will you apply this scripture to your life?

Detox Day 5   Date:

Meditation Scripture:

Proverbs 4:23 "Above all else, guard your heart,
for everything you do flows from it."

What boundaries do you need to set to help your
heart become pure?

____

____

What entertainment do you need to give up to help
your heart be pure?

____

____

What victories have you had in your purity today?

____

____

____

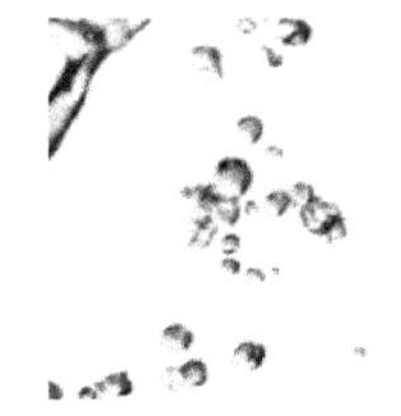

Detox Day 5

Date:

Meditation Scripture:

*Proverbs 4:23 "Above all else, guard your heart,
for everything you do flows from it."*

What failures do you need to confess today?

____
____
____

What temptations are you facing and praying about today?

____
____
____
____
____

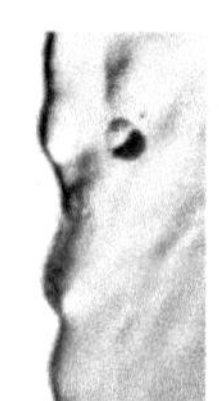

Detox Day 5   Date:

Meditation Scripture:

Proverbs 4:23 "Above all else, guard your heart,
for everything you do flows from it."

How do you feel about the conversation you had
with your detox partner/group today?

____
____

____

Take time to write out your thoughts and prayers to
God about your purity.

____
____
____
____

I want to encourage you that you made an amazing
and godly decision to persevere in your purity today
Keep striving for godliness. God will strengthen you!
Keep Going!

Detox Day 6   Date:

Meditation Scripture:

Matthew 5:8 "Blessed are the pure in heart,
for they will see God."

What does this scripture show you about yourself?

How will you apply this scripture to your life?

Detox Day 6   Date:

Meditation Scripture:

*Matthew 5:8 "Blessed are the pure in heart,
for they will see God."*

What boundaries do you need to set to help your
heart become pure?

____

____

What entertainment do you need to give up to help
your heart be pure?

____

____

What victories have you had in your purity today?

____

____

____

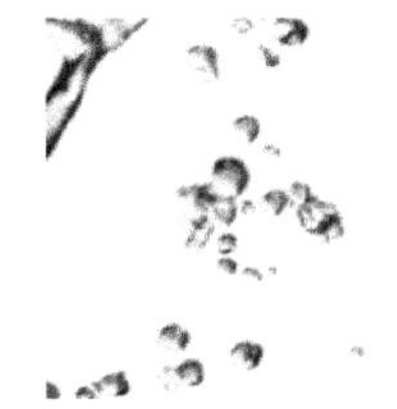  

Detox Day 6   Date:

Meditation Scripture:

*Matthew 5:8 "Blessed are the pure in heart,
for they will see God."*

What failures do you need to confess today?

____

____

What temptations are you facing and praying about today?

____

____

____

____

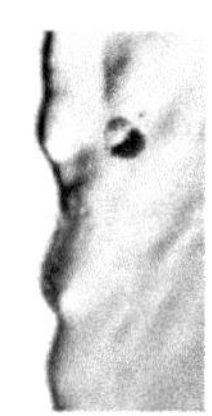

Detox Day 6

Date:

Meditation Scripture:

*Matthew 5:8 "Blessed are the pure in heart,
for they will see God."*

How do you feel about the conversation you had
with your detox partner/group today?

____

____

____

Take time to write out your thoughts and prayers to
God about your purity.

____

____

____

____

I want to encourage you that you made an amazing
and godly decision to persevere in your purity today
Keep striving for godliness. God will strengthen you!
Keep Going!

Detox Day 7

Date:

Meditation Scripture:

2 Tim 2:22 "Flee the evil desires of youth and pursue righteousness, faith, love and peace, along with those who call on the Lord out of a pure heart."

What does this scripture show you about yourself?

How will you apply this scripture to your life?

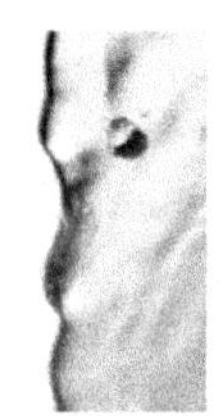

Detox Day 7   Date:

Meditation Scripture:

2 Tim 2:22 "Flee the evil desires of youth and pursue righteousness, faith, love and peace, along with those who call on the Lord out of a pure heart."

What boundaries do you need to set to help your heart become pure?

____

____

What entertainment do you need to give up to help your heart be pure?

____

____

What victories have you had in your purity today?

____

____

____

Detox Day 7

Date:

Meditation Scripture:

2 Tim 2:22 "Flee the evil desires of youth and pursue righteousness, faith, love and peace, along with those who call on the Lord out of a pure heart."

What failures do you need to confess today?

____

____

What temptations are you facing and praying about today?

____

____

____

____

____

Detox Day 7   Date:

Meditation Scripture:

2 Tim 2:22 "Flee the evil desires of youth and pursue righteousness, faith, love and peace, along with those who call on the Lord out of a pure heart."

How do you feel about the conversation you had with your detox partner/group today?

____

____

Take time to write out your thoughts and prayers to God about your purity.

____

____

____

I want to encourage you that you made an amazing and godly decision to persevere in your purity today Keep striving for godliness. God will strengthen you!
Keep Going!

Chapter Eight
Detoxing The Mind

"Those who live according to the flesh have their minds set on what the flesh desires; but those who live in accordance with the Spirit have their minds set on what the Spirit desires."

Romans 8:5-6

We have all heard of the saying "a mind is a terrible thing to waste". Imagine what the creator of man thinks when we allow our minds to be consumed with sinful thoughts and impurity instead of thinking about ways to glorify him. God wants us to think of godly things with our beautifully created minds. The opening scripture for this chapter speaks of the mind being either set on what the flesh desires or what the Spirit desires. When we are determined to please and love God then our minds will be set on figuring out how to do just that, but when we are determined to please the flesh and we feel entitled to that pleasure then our minds will inevitably be set on finding that pleasure. In this chapter we will focus on the very rarely discussed command to love God with all our mind.

Loving God with All Our Mind

Let us look at Matthew 22:37...

Jesus replied: " 'Love the Lord your God with all your heart and with all your soul and with all your mind"

The command in Matthew 22:37 is one of the most quoted scriptures. This scripture is also what Jesus calls the greatest commandment. We often hear this verse being shared with focus and emphasis on the "with all your heart" part of the verse. If we're careful we pay attention to the fact that God did not put more emphasis on the "with all your heart" part of this scripture than he put on the "with all your mind" part of it. Ask yourself, "am I loving God with all of my mind?". The mind is where our thinking happens so a simple way of examining whether we are loving God with all of our mind is by looking at our thought life. If the thoughts we are entertaining are not pure then we know the answer is "No, we're not loving God with all of our mind". God said to love him is to obey him. Therefore, the only way we will love God with our mind is by obeying him in our thoughts. This doesn't mean that if we love God then impure thoughts will never enter our minds. The enemy will always tempt us with impure thoughts. The choice we face is whether we will allow the thoughts Satan throws our way to become full blown movies in our mind or if we will take those thoughts captive.

Let us look at 2 Corinthians 10:5...

"We demolish arguments and every pretension that sets itself up against the knowledge of God, and we take captive every thought to make it obedient to Christ."

When we look at 2 Corinthians 10:5 we see that Paul explains that one of the ways we fight spiritually is by taking any thought that is against the truth and making it obedient to Christ. This is the way we must treat thoughts of impurity and lust if we want to detoxify our minds. We can't feast on impure thoughts and expect to be victorious in sexual purity. We must fight impure thoughts by seizing them when they come and challenging them with the word of God.

Detoxifying Our Minds

I understand that turning off thoughts of lust can seem to be impossible, especially if you have allowed yourself to indulge in lustful thoughts consistently. There is an old saying that I've found to be true which is "if you give Satan an inch, then he will take a mile.". It's a scheme of Satan to convince us that a few little impure thoughts aren't too bad. If we'll be honest, we'll admit that our mind never stops at a few little dirty thoughts. Those few little thoughts become full blown movies in our mind and if we don't stop them those movies lead to sexual arousal and sexual arousal is a powerful feeling that is hard to shut down without some form of sexual activity. Our thought life is where purity begins and ends. Yes, the bible says sexually immoral thoughts come from within a man's heart and that is true; However, if we control our thoughts, we will not end up acting out the sinful desires of our heart.

When was the last time you did anything without having to think about doing it first? I imagine you answered "never" and to that I agree. This is the order of things; our actions follow our thoughts. Our thoughts come from things that are in our hearts, but those things which are in our hearts don't get "activated" until they reach our minds. I once heard it said this way, "the mind's job is to work 24/7 to bring about what the heart desires.".

Let us look at Matthew 15:19...

"For out of the heart come evil thoughts—murder, adultery, sexual immorality, theft, false testimony, slander."

Let us also look at Matthew 9:4...

"Knowing their thoughts, Jesus said, "Why do you entertain evil thoughts in your hearts?"

Matthew 15:19 tells us that thoughts about sexual immorality come from within our hearts. In last week's detox we focused on how to detox our hearts. We removed spiritual toxins from our lives and set boundaries to help guard our hearts from contamination. The steps we took to guard our hearts last week will help us to detoxify our minds as well.

As we read Matthew 9:4 let us pay attention to the operative word "entertain". Jesus asked them why they entertain the evil thoughts in their hearts. Jesus didn't just ask them "why did you have those thoughts?". Imagine Jesus asking you this same question about the sexually impure thoughts you've had. What if Jesus asked you ___________(insert your name), why do you entertain lustful thoughts in your heart? How would you respond? God knows that the enemy will tempt us with impure thoughts. God does not call us to not be tempted, he calls us to not give in to temptation. The reason it is key for us to pay attention to the word "entertain" is because we must get the fact that entertaining impure thoughts is the opposite of taking them captive. If these guys had taken their thoughts captive and challenged them with the truth, then they would not have been in the wrong. Learning to take our thoughts captive is going to be vital in detoxifying our minds.

Changing Your Mind Changes Your Life

As followers of Christ the goal is for us to become more like Christ. If we want to become like Christ, then we must learn to take note of how Christ thinks. We will never know the actual private thoughts of Jesus' mind, but we know how he thought because we see how he lived. Jesus is perfect and therefore he was incapable of living in a way that wasn't a true reflection of the way he thought. 1 Peter 2:22 says, *"He committed no sin, and no deceit was found in his mouth.".* When we look at the decisions and behaviors of Jesus then we should make up our minds to make the same types of decisions he made and to behave the way he did. It's not possible for us to become like Jesus without giving up worldly thinking. If we have been allowing our minds to be set on lust and sexual sin then we have been hindering ourselves from becoming like Christ.

We cannot compartmentalize impurities. Impurity is pervasive. Even when we think we are separating our sexual sin from other areas of our lives we are not. A sexually impure thought life is inevitably going to pollute the other areas of our lives in some way. Living a life of indulging in sexual impurity in our minds while performing like "Christians" in other areas of our lives will weigh us down with guilt and if left unchecked eventually lead us to being hardened and desensitized to sexual sin. The godly response to sin is repentance. If we become desensitized to sin, then our minds start to accept sin as "normal stuff" and our hearts lose our urgency to repent. Living in sexual sin hinders us from truly being the person God has called us to be which means that we can't truly live our lives right as a whole. God does not accept selective obedience. God looks at us in whole and he calls us to love him with ALL of our heart, ALL of our strength and ALL or our mind.

In order to detoxify our minds of sexual sin we have to give up the idea that impure thoughts are acceptable and take on Gods' way of thinking about impurity.

Let us look at Romans 12:2...

"Do not conform to the pattern of this world but be transformed by the renewing of your mind. Then you will be able to test and approve what God's will is—his good, pleasing and perfect will."

Let us also look at Philippians 2:5...

"In your relationships with one another, have the same mindset as Christ Jesus."

Lastly, let us look at Colossians 3:10...

"...since you have taken off your old self with its practices and have put on the new self, which is being renewed in knowledge in the image of its Creator."

The message we get from looking at Romans 12:2 is that the way we will change who we are is by changing the way we think. This verse did not say be transformed by reading your bible and it didn't say be transformed by doing good things. No, it says be transformed by renewing your mind. Reading our bibles and doing good are vital parts of changing, but true change starts in changing our minds. We have more power to change by changing the way we think than we have by trying to change from the outside in. Let's also pay attention to the beginning of this verse which tells us to stop conforming to the ways of the world. The world says that it's normal to live in sexual sin. The world promotes sexual sin. The world even attempts to convince us to focus on the pleasure of sexual sin with no regard to the physical, emotional, and spiritual consequences of sexual sin. In contrast, not only does God's word tell us to avoid sexual sin but it also warns us of the consequences of it. I often say, "ignorance is the devil's hiding place." Ignorance is the opposite of knowledge. Gaining knowledge of what God's word says is how we renew our minds. Taking on that knowledge as our new way of thinking is how we begin to transform.

Philippians 2:5 calls us to have the mind of Christ in our relationships with one another. Sexual sin always has to have someone to focus on and to feast on. No matter what kind of sexual sin is being committed it always involves another person. If it is intercourse then clearly there is another person involved, if it is self-sex then another person is being thought about during the act, if it is porn then another person is being watched, if it is lustful thoughts another person is being fantasized about. I encourage you to reconcile the call for us to have the mind of Christ in our relationships with one another to having lustful and impure thoughts about each other. Though that verse is written to teach the church to imitate Christs' humility we know that the call to imitate him is for all situations. When we are thinking impure thoughts about another person, we are in no way imitating Christ. Christ came so that all people can be saved. When we think about people, we need to think about them the way that Christ would no matter what they are wearing, doing, or taking part in.

Lastly, studying Colossians 3:10 brings us deeper into our understanding that it is by the knowledge of God that we are renewed. Meditating on God's word day and night will feed our minds with more and more knowledge about who God is and what God says. The knowledge of who Christ is and who he calls us to be will empower us to fight against the enemy when he is trying to tempt us to conform to the ways of the world.

Let us Start Week 2!

During the next seven days of this detox, we are going to focus heavily on detoxing our thought life.

I encourage you to write down as many of your thoughts as possible. After writing down your thoughts you will find scriptures that help you bring those thoughts into obedience to Christ. It will serve you well to be open and honest with your detox partner about the thoughts you are having. You want to be wise and not share names or any unnecessary details about your thoughts. It will also help you to ask your detox partner for their feedback after sharing your thoughts with them.

I hope this week's detox leads you into an abundance of refreshment and freedom in your thought life.

To God's glory!

Let me pray for your week!

Heavenly Father, I come to you in Jesus' name praying for the person who is reading this book right now. I pray that you will strengthen their mind in a way that the enemy will no longer be able to use their mind against you, Father God in Heaven. I pray that they will develop such a love for your word that their minds will become fortified with your word in a way that makes it hard for the enemy to get a thought into their mind. I pray for them to have an amazing week doing the detox this week and that they gain greater convictions about thinking pure thoughts than they could ask, think, or imagine. I pray for the enemy to be kicked out of their minds. I pray that their mind will be renewed and that they will no longer find sinful and lustful thoughts to be acceptable, pleasurable, or comfortable. I ask this in Jesus' name.

Week 2 Purity Goals

What is something you want to avoid doing for this entire week? (e.g., entertaining impure thoughts)

____

____

What scripture are you going to use to help fight the temptation to do the thing(s) you listed above?

____

____

At the end of this week come back here and tell how you did in reaching this goal this week.

____

____

Detox Day 8   Date:

Meditation Scripture:

Colossians 3:2 "Set your minds on things above, not on earthly things"

What does this scripture show you about yourself?

____

____

____

____

____

____

____

____

How will you apply this scripture to your life?

____

____

____

____

Detox Day 8

Date:

Meditation Scripture:

Colossians 3:2 "Set your minds on things above, not on earthly things"

What boundaries do you need to set to help your mind become pure?

What entertainment do you need to give up to help your mind be pure?

What victories have you had in your purity today?

Detox Day 8   Date:

Meditation Scripture:

Colossians 3:2 "Set your minds on things above, not on earthly things"

What failures do you need to confess today?

____

____

What temptations are you facing and praying about today?

____

____

____

____

....

Detox Day 8

Date:

Meditation Scripture:

Colossians 3:2 "Set your minds on things above, not on earthly things"

What thoughts are you fighting to take captive today?

Write down three scriptures that will help you fight against the thoughts you listed above.

Detox Day 8   Date:

Meditation Scripture:

Colossians 3:2 "Set your minds on things above, not on earthly things"

How do you feel about the conversation you had
with your detox partner/group today?

____

____

____

Take time to write out your thoughts and prayers to
God about your purity.

____

____

____

____

I want to encourage you that you made an amazing
and godly decision to persevere in your purity today
Keep striving for godliness. God will strengthen you!
Keep Going!

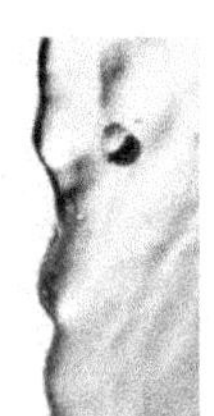

Detox Day 9   Date:

What does this scripture show you about yourself?

____

____

____

____

____

____

____

How will you apply this scripture to your life?

____

____

____

____

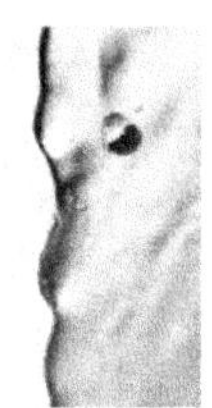

Detox Day 9

Date:

Meditation Scripture:

Romans 8:5-6 "For those who live according to the flesh set their minds on the things of the flesh, but those who live according to the Spirit set their minds on the things of the Spirit."

What boundaries do you need to set to help your mind become pure?

____

____

____

What entertainment do you need to give up to help your mind be pure?

____

____

What victories have you had in your purity today?

____

____

____

Detox Day 9   Date:

Meditation Scripture:

Romans 8:5-6 "For those who live according to the flesh set their minds on the things of the flesh, but those who live according to the Spirit set their minds on the things of the Spirit."

What failures do you need to confess today?

____

____

____

What temptations are you facing and praying about today?

____

____

____

____

____

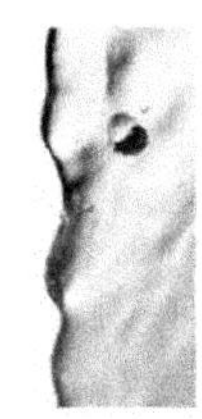

Detox Day 9

Date:

Meditation Scripture:

Romans 8:5-6 "For those who live according to the flesh set their minds on the things of the flesh, but those who live according to the Spirit set their minds on the things of the Spirit."

What thoughts are you fighting to take captive today?

Write down three scriptures that will help you fight against the thoughts you listed above.

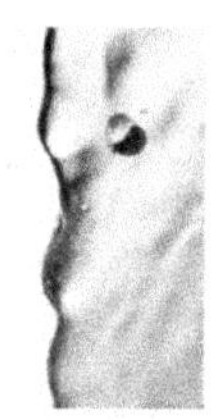

Detox Day 9   Date:

Meditation Scripture:

Romans 8:5-6 "For those who live according to the flesh set their minds on the things of the flesh, but those who live according to the Spirit set their minds on the things of the Spirit."

How do you feel about the conversation you had with your detox partner/group today?

____

____

____

Take time to write out your thoughts and prayers to God about your purity.

____

____

____

____

I want to encourage you that you made an amazing and godly decision to persevere in your purity today Keep striving for godliness. God will strengthen you!
Keep Going!

Detox Day 10

Date:

Meditation Scripture:

Proverbs 15:26 "The Lord detests the thoughts of the wicked, but those of the pure are pleasing to him."

What does this scripture show you about yourself?

How will you apply this scripture to your life?

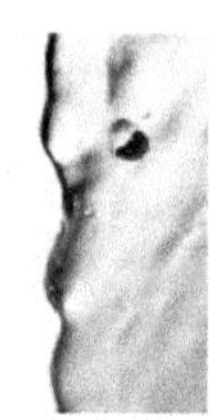

Detox Day 10

Date:

Meditation Scripture:

Proverbs 15:26 "The Lord detests the thoughts of the wicked, but those of the pure are pleasing to him."

What boundaries do you need to set to help your mind become pure?

____

____

____

What entertainment do you need to give up to help your mind be pure?

____

____

What victories have you had in your purity today?

____

____

____

  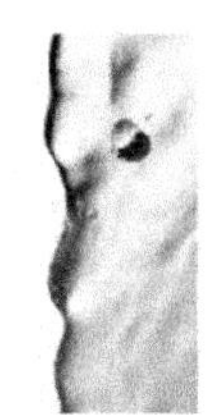

Detox Day 10

Date:

Meditation Scripture:

Proverbs 15:26 "The Lord detests the thoughts of the wicked, but those of the pure are pleasing to him."

What failures do you need to confess today?

____

____

____

What temptations are you facing and praying about today?

____

____

____

____

____

Detox Day 10

Date:

Meditation Scripture:

Proverbs 15:26 "The Lord detests the thoughts of the wicked, but those of the pure are pleasing to him."

What thoughts are you fighting to take captive today?

____

____

____

Write down three scriptures that will help you fight against the thoughts you listed above.

____

____

____

____

____

  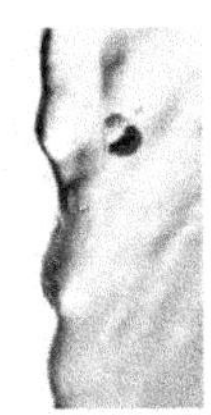

Detox Day 10   Date:

Meditation Scripture:

Proverbs 15:26 "The Lord detests the thoughts of the wicked, but those of the pure are pleasing to him."

How do you feel about the conversation you had with your detox partner/group today?

____

____

____

Take time to write out your thoughts and prayers to God about your purity.

____

____

____

____

I want to encourage you that you made an amazing and godly decision to persevere in your purity today Keep striving for godliness. God will strengthen you!
Keep Going!

Detox Day 11   Date:

Meditation Scripture:

Colossians 3:5 "Put to death, therefore, whatever belongs to your earthly nature: sexual immorality, impurity, lust, evil desires and greed, which is idolatry"

What does this scripture show you about yourself?

____

____

____

____

____

____

____

How will you apply this scripture to your life?

____

____

____

____

Detox Day 11   Date:

Meditation Scripture:

Colossians 3:5 "Put to death, therefore, whatever belongs to your earthly nature: sexual immorality, impurity, lust, evil desires and greed, which is idolatry"

What boundaries do you need to set to help your mind become pure?

____

____

____

What entertainment do you need to give up to help your mind be pure?

____

____

What victories have you had in your purity today?

____

____

____

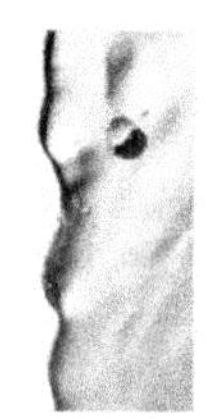

Detox Day 11   Date:

Meditation Scripture:

Colossians 3:5 "Put to death, therefore, whatever belongs to your earthly nature: sexual immorality, impurity, lust, evil desires and greed, which is idolatry"

What failures do you need to confess today?

____

____

____

What temptations are you facing and praying about today?

____

____

____

____

____

Detox Day 11   Date:

Meditation Scripture:

Colossians 3:5 "Put to death, therefore, whatever belongs to your earthly nature: sexual immorality, impurity, lust, evil desires and greed, which is idolatry"

What thoughts are you fighting to take captive today?

____

____

Write down three scriptures that will help you fight against the thoughts you listed above.

____

____

____

____

____

Detox Day 11   Date:

Meditation Scripture:

Colossians 3:5 "Put to death, therefore, whatever belongs to your earthly nature: sexual immorality, impurity, lust, evil desires and greed, which is idolatry"

How do you feel about the conversation you had with your detox partner/group today?

____

____

____

Take time to write out your thoughts and prayers to God about your purity.

____

____

____

____

I want to encourage you that you made an amazing and godly decision to persevere in your purity today Keep striving for godliness. God will strengthen you! Keep Going!

Detox Day 12   Date:

What does this scripture show you about yourself?

How will you apply this scripture to your life?

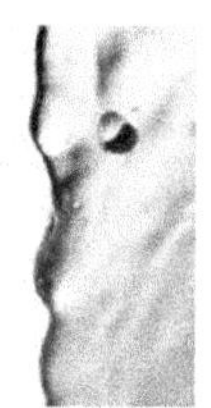

Detox Day 12

Date:

Meditation Scripture:

1 John 2:16 "For everything in the world—the lust of the flesh, the lust of the eyes, and the pride of life—comes not from the Father but from the world."

What boundaries do you need to set to help your mind become pure?

____

____

What entertainment do you need to give up to help your mind be pure?

____

____

What victories have you had in your purity today?

____

____

____

Detox Day 12   Date:

Meditation Scripture:

1 John 2:16 "For everything in the world—the lust of the flesh, the lust of the eyes, and the pride of life—comes not from the Father but from the world."

What failures do you need to confess today?

____

____

____

What temptations are you facing and praying about today?

____

____

____

____

____

Detox Day 12   Date:

Meditation Scripture:

1 John 2:16 "For everything in the world—the lust of the flesh, the lust of the eyes, and the pride of life—comes not from the Father but from the world."

What thoughts are you fighting to take captive today?

____

____

____

Write down three scriptures that will help you fight against the thoughts you listed above.

____

____

____

____

____

Detox Day 12   Date:

How do you feel about the conversation you had with your detox partner/group today?

____

____

____

Take time to write out your thoughts and prayers to God about your purity.

____

____

____

____

I want to encourage you that you made an amazing and godly decision to persevere in your purity today Keep striving for godliness. God will strengthen you!
Keep Going!

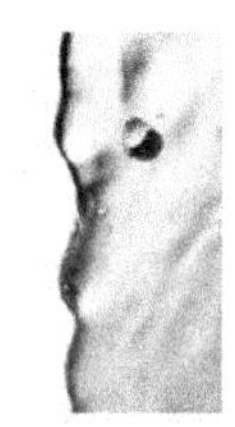

Detox Day 13   Date:

Meditation Scripture:

Philippians 4:8 "...whatever is true, whatever is noble, whatever is right, whatever is pure, whatever is lovely, whatever is admirable—if anything is excellent or praiseworthy—think about such things.

What does this scripture show you about yourself?

How will you apply this scripture to your life?

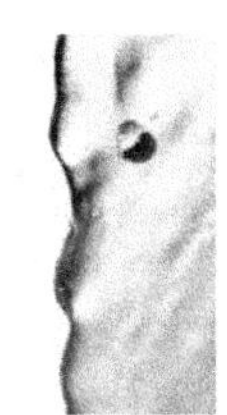

Detox Day 13   Date:

Meditation Scripture:

Philippians 4:8 "...whatever is true, whatever is noble, whatever is right, whatever is pure, whatever is lovely, whatever is admirable—if anything is excellent or praiseworthy—think about such things.

What boundaries do you need to set to help your mind become pure?

____

____

What entertainment do you need to give up to help your mind be pure?

____

____

What victories have you had in your purity today?

____

____

____

Detox Day 13

Date:

Meditation Scripture:

Philippians 4:8 "...whatever is true, whatever is noble, whatever is right, whatever is pure, whatever is lovely, whatever is admirable—if anything is excellent or praiseworthy—think about such things.

What failures do you need to confess today?

What temptations are you facing and praying about today?

Detox Day 13   Date:

Meditation Scripture:

Philippians 4:8 "...whatever is true, whatever is noble, whatever is right, whatever is pure, whatever is lovely, whatever is admirable—if anything is excellent or praiseworthy—think about such things.

What thoughts are you fighting to take captive today?

____

____

____

Write down three scriptures that will help you fight against the thoughts you listed above.

____

____

____

____

____

Detox Day 13   Date:

Meditation Scripture:

Philippians 4:8 "...whatever is true, whatever is noble, whatever is right, whatever is pure, whatever is lovely, whatever is admirable—if anything is excellent or praiseworthy—think about such things.

How do you feel about the conversation you had
with your detox partner/group today?

____

____

____

Take time to write out your thoughts and prayers to
God about your purity.

____

____

____

____

I want to encourage you that you made an amazing
and godly decision to persevere in your purity today
Keep striving for godliness. God will strengthen you!
Keep Going!

Detox Day 14   Date:

1 Corinthians 6:9 .."the unrighteous will not inherit the kingdom of God? Do not be deceived: neither the sexually immoral, nor idolaters, nor adulterers, nor men who practice homosexuality..."

What does this scripture show you about yourself?

How will you apply this scripture to your life?

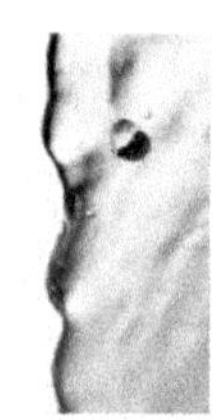

Detox Day 14   Date:

Meditation Scripture:

*1 Corinthians 6:9 .."the unrighteous will not inherit the kingdom of God?
Do not be deceived: neither the sexually immoral, nor idolaters, nor
adulterers, nor men who practice homosexuality..."*

What boundaries do you need to set to help your
mind become pure?

____

____

What entertainment do you need to give up to help
your mind be pure?

____

____

What victories have you had in your purity today?

____

____

____

  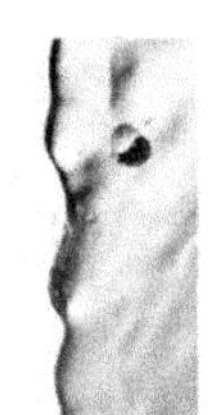

Detox Day 14   Date:

Meditation Scripture:

*1 Corinthians 6:9 .."the unrighteous will not inherit the kingdom of God?
Do not be deceived: neither the sexually immoral, nor idolaters, nor
adulterers, nor men who practice homosexuality..."*

What failures do you need to confess today?

____

____

What temptations are you facing and praying about today?

____

____

____

____

Detox Day 14

Date:

Meditation Scripture:

1 Corinthians 6:9 .."the unrighteous will not inherit the kingdom of God? Do not be deceived: neither the sexually immoral, nor idolaters, nor adulterers, nor men who practice homosexuality..."

What thoughts are you fighting to take captive today?

____

____

____

Write down three scriptures that will help you fight against the thoughts you listed above.

____

____

____

____

____

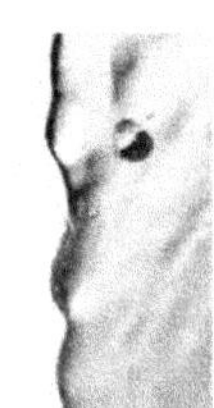

Detox Day 14   Date:

Meditation Scripture:

*1 Corinthians 6:9 .."the unrighteous will not inherit the kingdom of God?
Do not be deceived: neither the sexually immoral, nor idolaters, nor
adulterers, nor men who practice homosexuality..."*

How do you feel about the conversation you had
with your detox partner/group today?

____

____

Take time to write out your thoughts and prayers to
God about your purity.

____

____

____

____

I want to encourage you that you made an amazing
and godly decision to persevere in your purity today
Keep striving for godliness. God will strengthen you!
Keep Going!

Chapter Nine

Detoxing The Body

"Therefore, I urge you, brothers and sisters, in view of God's mercy, to offer your bodies as a living sacrifice, holy and pleasing to God—this is your true and proper worship."

Romans 12:1

Finally, we will focus on detoxing the body! The biggest step we'll need to take in detoxing the body is to make up our minds to stop doing anything sexually inappropriate. If you are married of course this means you only need to stop doing anything sexual that violates God's standard of keeping your marriage bed pure. Having sex with someone we are not married to is sin.

Some people have argued that the bible does not exactly say that we should not have sex outside of marriage, but Gods' word makes it very clear that sex is only pure when it is between a woman and a man who are married to each other. In this chapter we will look at what God's word does say about waiting until we are married to have sex. Some of us want to have our cake and eat it too, but if we want life with God then we must surrender our desires to God. It's a common practice for people to be in a sexually immoral relationship while saying they are following Jesus. Practicing purity as Christians is not optional. Purity is what all who follow Jesus are called to.

As we see in the opening scripture for this chapter, God calls us to use our bodies in ways that are holy and pleasing to him. If we are honest most of us can't convince ourselves to say that having sex outside of marriage even feels holy and pleasing to God. Sexual immorality is pleasing to our bodies, but it is definitely not pleasing to God. If we want to please God we have to choose to please him over pleasing ourselves. We not only have to stop having actual intercourse we must stop any act that is not holy and pleasing to God. In today's world there is a movement of people who believe that having oral sex and masturbating is not as wrong as having sexual intercourse. Studying God's word reveals to us that any sexual act outside of marriage is sin.

I imagine that for some people the idea of not doing anything sexual is incredibly challenging. The beauty of living according to God's standard is that there is always a blessing in it for us. While you journey through these last seven days of this detox you will focus on the ways that abstaining from sexual sin blesses you. God is good and every command he has for us is for our good

Let us look at 1st Corinthians 6:18 - 20 ...

*"Flee from sexual immorality. All other sins a person commits are outside the body, but whoever sins sexually, sins against their own body. Do you not know that your bodies are temples of the Holy Spirit, who is in you, whom you have received from God? You are not your own; **you** were bought at a price. Therefore honor God with your bodies."*

Let us also look at Colossians 3:5 ...

"Put to death, therefore, whatever belongs to your earthly nature: sexual immorality, impurity, lust, evil desires and greed, which is idolatry."

Let's also look at 1 Corinthians 7:8-9 ...

"So I say to those who aren't married and to widows—it's better to stay unmarried, just as I am. But if they can't control themselves, they should go ahead and marry. It's better to marry than to burn with lust."

Lastly, let us look at Matthew 5:27-28 ...

"You have heard the commandment that says, 'You must not commit adultery.' But I say, anyone who even looks at a woman with lust has already committed adultery with her in his heart."

As we read 1 Corinthians 6:18-20 we see that our bodies don't even belong to us. Once we are in Christ our bodies have now become the temple of the Holy Spirit. Imagine you have moved into a house, and you've paid for it in full, but the previous owner is still coming over to have sex in your new house. That would be wild, bizarre, and completely inappropriate to say the least. Ask yourself if you would feel violated if this happened to you. When we accept Jesus as Lord of our lives, we are giving our bodies to him for the housing of the Holy Spirit. Therefore, when we sin sexually, we now sin against the temple of the Holy Spirit. Most of us would agree that having sex inside of an actual brick and mortar church building would never be an option due to our reverence for God. How much more should we have a reverence for God about committing sexual sin in the very house of the Holy Spirit which is our bodies. If we have more concern about sinning at the brick-and-mortar building than in our own bodies, then we must ask ourselves do we have more respect for a building "across town" than we do for our ever-present friend, the Holy Spirit? He lives in us.

Looking at Colossians 3:5 helps us to understand that we can't continue to have sex as unmarried people after we give our lives to Christ. When we come to Christ, we have decided that we are going to give up our earthly and worldly behaviors to please God. Giving up sexual sin needs to be an immediate decision even though bringing our bodies into submission to that decision will be a process. It's no secret that nobody is perfect, but God calls us to not be imperfect on purpose. We will experience temptation to sin sexually, but we can't use feeling tempted as justification to live a sexually immoral life. We must reach for God's ever extended hand for help and he will strengthen us in the face of temptation. At times we can feel as if we are alone in our struggles against sexual sin and that is why it is important to have spiritual partners in our lives whom we can be honest with about our struggles. Continuing to use the tools which we are using in this detox will help us to be victorious in putting to death the things that belong to our earthly nature.

1st Corinthians 7:8-9 speaks about the unmarried people who can no longer refrain from lust needing to go ahead and get married. Let us break this scripture down a little. If Paul had to tell unmarried people to go ahead and get married instead of burning in lust, then it's clear that the standard was for them to not be having sex before they got married. To further the point, Paul did not say "it's better to just go ahead and have sex" he said "go ahead and get married". Why didn't Paul tell them to just go ahead and have sex? Could it be because God had already made it clear that sex before marriage is sin? As singles the most important thing we can take away from this scripture is that sex is supposed to only be had in marriage and only in marriage. Step one in us detoxing our bodies is accepting this standard and discontinuing any sexual acts in which we are involved.

Last but not least, as we meditate on Matthew 5:28-29 we get perspective on how God feels about pornography. We have to want to make the connection between this scripture and what it shows us about watching pornography in order to see the connection. When this scripture was written there were no televisions or recording devices therefore pornographic videos didn't exist. Let's look at how we reconcile watching pornography to what Gods' word says in this scripture. Jesus said that if someone even looks at a woman lustfully, they have committed adultery. Imagine what Jesus' response would have been to a person looking at people's naked bodies on a screen. Now let's take it a step higher, what would Jesus say about us watching two people have sex in movies. If we really get honest, we can see that even watching "soft porn" scenes in regular movies and shows can be challenged by this scripture. The world is full of opportunities to watch inappropriate content, but those same opportunities are opportunities for us to choose God by turning away from viewing those things. Matthew 6:22-23 says, *"Your eye is like a lamp that provides light for your body. When your eye is healthy, your whole body is filled with light. But when your eye is unhealthy, your whole body is filled with darkness.* " We see here in Matthew 6:22-23 that our eyes are what lead the way for us. If our physical eyes are not working well then how do we get to where we need to go in our physical lives. The same is to be understood about our eyes when it comes to our spiritual lives. If we are watching pornography how is that guiding our hearts and minds down the path to sexual purity? Knowing this, we must be very careful about what we watch because what we focus on with our eyes will inevitably impact our spiritual direction. Our eyes are part of our holy temples too, so we need to keep our eyes pure.

During this week's detox we will focus on detoxing our bodies. Our bodies are the precious temple of the Holy Spirit, and we should treat them as if the Holy Spirit lives in us.

Let us Start Week 3!

I hope that by now you are experiencing refreshment from reading what God's word says about sexual purity.

At this point you should be on day fifteen of your fast. It has likely been a challenge at times to stay committed to your fast, but it's worth it to persevere. My prayer for anyone reading this book is that God will grant you the strength to finish your fast.

In these last seven days of this detox we will focus on removing things that are causing us to sin sexually and we will also focus on setting boundaries with any person(s) who is causing us to struggle in our purity.

Just as in the previous chapters, it is important for you to stay very honest and open with your detox partner about your answers to this week's journal questions. It can be tempting to keep relationships that we know are not good for us a secret. We don't want to give up the comfort we get from having those relationships, but it is vital that we bring these types of situations to light. I encourage you to take the powerful step of speaking out to your detox partner about any compromising situations and relationships you've been involved in. It will take courage for you to talk about these things, but you will be so glad you did once you experience the refreshment that comes from repentance. God wants all of you and I hope you use the next seven days to make every effort to give him just that, your all!

This week you will have two meditation scriptures for each day. I encourage you to write them both down and take them with you so that you can meditate on them throughout your day. It may even help to type them into a text or email that can be sent to you automatically at specific times of the day. The purpose here is to help you to put the word of God in your heart and mind so that you can stand against the temptations you face.

I'm hoping and genuinely praying for you to grow closer to God through this time of fasting, studying Gods' word, and detoxifying your body!

Let me pray for your week!

Father God in Heaven we come to you in Jesus' name. I am praying for the person who is reading this book right now that you will strengthen them like never before in their purity. I pray for them to have the strength in their innermost being to repent of anything they need to repent of so that times of refreshing may come. I pray for them to have a paradigm shift that will bring them into making choices in their purity which align with your word and your will for their lives. I pray that this week they have the courage to be completely honest and open about their struggles and about any sin and situations they have been involved in. I pray for them to feel your grace and to accept it and appreciate it. I pray that they feel your love and that knowing you love them will keep them motivated to stay faithful to you. I pray for them to experience victory in their sexual purity in all the ways that have felt impossible. Your word says through you all things are possible. I pray that they may have peace in knowing that Jesus died for their sins and that no matter what sins they have committed he has already paid the price for their forgiveness. I pray this in the name of our Lord and savior Jesus Christ.

Week 3 Purity Goals

What is something you want to avoid doing for this entire week? (e.g., entertaining impure thoughts)

What scripture are you going to use to help fight the temptation to do the thing(s) you listed above?

At the end of this week come back here and tell how you did in reaching this goal this week.

Detox Day 15   Date:

Meditation Scriptures:

Romans 13:14 "Let every part of you belong to the Lord Jesus Christ. Do not allow your weak thoughts to lead you into sinful actions."

Colossians 3:2 "Keep your minds thinking about things in heaven. Do not think about things on the earth."

What is God saying to you in today's meditation scriptures?

____
____
____
____
____
____
____
____
____
____

Detox Day 15

Date:

Meditation Scriptures:

Romans 13:14 "Let every part of you belong to the Lord Jesus Christ. Do not allow your weak thoughts to lead you into sinful actions."

Colossians 3:2 "Keep your minds thinking about things in heaven. Do not think about things on the earth."

What things do you need to give up in order to honor God with your body?

____

____

____

____

____

____

____

____

____

____

Detox Day 15

Date:

Meditation Scriptures:

Romans 13:14 "Let every part of you belong to the Lord Jesus Christ. Do not allow your weak thoughts to lead you into sinful actions."

Colossians 3:2 "Keep your minds thinking about things in heaven. Do not think about things on the earth."

What relationships do you need to set boundaries in to protect your purity?

____

____

____

What boundaries will you set in the relationships you listed above?

____

____

____

____

____

Detox Day 15   Date:

Meditation Scriptures:

Romans 13:14 "Let every part of you belong to the Lord Jesus Christ. Do not allow your weak thoughts to lead you into sinful actions."

Colossians 3:2 "Keep your minds thinking about things in heaven. Do not think about things on the earth."

Write a list of any inappropriate content that you need to stop watching.

____

____

____

What will you do when you are tempted to watch the content you listed above?

____

____

____

____

Detox Day 15   Date:

Meditation Scriptures:

Romans 13:14 "Let every part of you belong to the Lord Jesus Christ. Do not allow your weak thoughts to lead you into sinful actions."

Colossians 3:2 "Keep your minds thinking about things in heaven. Do not think about things on the earth."

Are there any sins you've committed against your body that you need to confess?

____

____

____

What temptations have you faced in your sexual purity today?

____

____

____

____

____

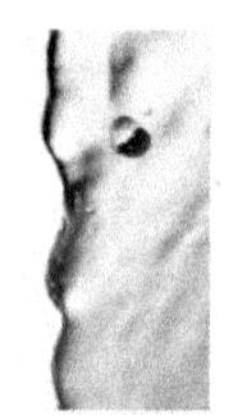

Detox Day 15   Date:

Meditation Scriptures:

Romans 13:14 "Let every part of you belong to the Lord Jesus Christ. Do not allow your weak thoughts to lead you into sinful actions."

Colossians 3:2 "Keep your minds thinking about things in heaven. Do not think about things on the earth."

What victories did you experience today?

____

____

____

____

What is your biggest takeaway from today's meditation scripture and journaling?

____

____

____

____

Detox Day 15   Date:

Meditation Scriptures:

Romans 13:14 "Let every part of you belong to the Lord Jesus Christ. Do not allow your weak thoughts to lead you into sinful actions."

Colossians 3:2 "Keep your minds thinking about things in heaven. Do not think about things on the earth."

Take time to write out your thoughts and prayers to God about your purity.

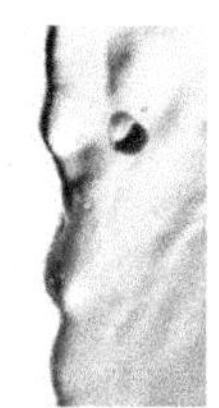

Detox Day 15   Date:

Meditation Scriptures:

Romans 13:14 "Let every part of you belong to the Lord Jesus Christ. Do not allow your weak thoughts to lead you into sinful actions."

Colossians 3:2 "Keep your minds thinking about things in heaven. Do not think about things on the earth."

How do you feel about the conversation you had
with your detox partner/group today?

____

____

____

____

____

____

____

I want to encourage you that you made an amazing
and godly decision to persevere in your purity today.
Keep striving for godliness. God will strengthen you!
Keep Going!

Detox Day 16   Date:

Meditation Scriptures:

Ephesians 5:3 "Do not let sex sins or anything sinful be even talked about among those who belong to Christ."

Galatians 5:16 "I say this to you: Let the Holy Spirit lead you in each step. Then you will not please your sinful old selves."

What is God saying to you in today's meditation scriptures?

____

____

____

____

____

____

____

____

____

Detox Day 16   Date:

Meditation Scriptures:

Ephesians 5:3 "Do not let sex sins or anything sinful be even talked about among those who belong to Christ."

Galatians 5:16 "I say this to you: Let the Holy Spirit lead you in each step. Then you will not please your sinful old selves."

What things do you need to give up in order to honor God with your body?

____

____

____

____

____

____

____

____

____

Detox Day 16   Date:

Meditation Scriptures:

Ephesians 5:3 "Do not let sex sins or anything sinful be even talked about among those who belong to Christ."

Galatians 5:16 "I say this to you: Let the Holy Spirit lead you in each step. Then you will not please your sinful old selves."

What relationships do you need to set boundaries in to protect your purity?

____

____

____

____

What boundaries will you set in the relationships you listed above?

____

____

____

____

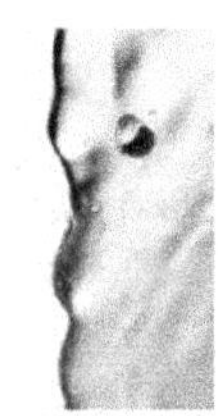

Detox Day 16

Date:

Meditation Scriptures:

Ephesians 5:3 "Do not let sex sins or anything sinful be even talked about among those who belong to Christ."

Galatians 5:16 "I say this to you: Let the Holy Spirit lead you in each step. Then you will not please your sinful old selves."

Write a list of any inappropriate content that you need to stop watching.

____

____

____

What will you do when you are tempted to watch the content you listed above?

____

____

____

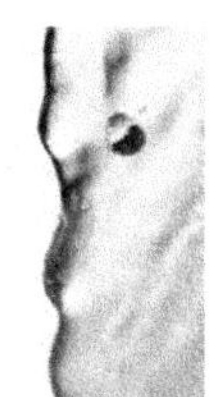

Detox Day 16   Date:

Meditation Scriptures:

Ephesians 5:3 "Do not let sex sins or anything sinful be even talked about among those who belong to Christ."

Galatians 5:16 "I say this to you: Let the Holy Spirit lead you in each step. Then you will not please your sinful old selves."

Are there any sins you've committed against your body that you need to confess?

____

____

____

What temptations have you faced in your sexual purity today?

____

____

____

____

____

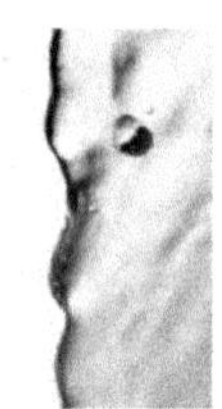

Detox Day 16

Date:

Meditation Scriptures:

Ephesians 5:3 "Do not let sex sins or anything sinful be even talked about among those who belong to Christ."

Galatians 5:16 "I say this to you: Let the Holy Spirit lead you in each step. Then you will not please your sinful old selves."

What victories did you experience today?

____

____

____

____

What is your biggest takeaway from today's meditation scripture and journaling?

____

____

____

____

  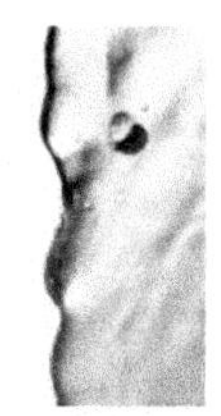

Detox Day 16   Date:

Meditation Scriptures:

Ephesians 5:3 "Do not let sex sins or anything sinful be even talked about among those who belong to Christ."

Galatians 5:16 "I say this to you: Let the Holy Spirit lead you in each step. Then you will not please your sinful old selves."

Take time to write out your thoughts and prayers to God about your purity.

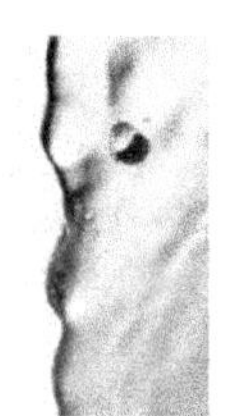

Detox Day 16   Date:

Meditation Scriptures:

Ephesians 5:3 "Do not let sex sins or anything sinful be even talked about among those who belong to Christ."

Galatians 5:16 "I say this to you: Let the Holy Spirit lead you in each step. Then you will not please your sinful old selves."

How do you feel about the conversation you had
with your detox partner/group today?

____

____

____

____

____

____

I want to encourage you that you made an amazing
and godly decision to persevere in your purity today.
Keep striving for godliness. God will strengthen you!
Keep Going!

Detox Day 17   Date:

Meditation Scriptures:

Galatians 6:6-7 "Do not be fooled. You cannot fool God. A man will get back whatever he plants! If a man does things to please his sinful old self, his soul will be lost. If a man does things to please the Holy Spirit, he will have life that lasts forever."

Ephesians 5:5 "Be sure of this! No person who does sex sins or who is not pure will have any part in the holy nation of Christ and of God."

What is God saying to you in today's meditation scriptures?

____
____
____
____
____
____
____
____
____

Detox Day 17

Date:

Meditation Scriptures:

Galatians 6:6-7 "Do not be fooled. You cannot fool God. A man will get back whatever he plants! If a man does things to please his sinful old self, his soul will be lost. If a man does things to please the Holy Spirit, he will have life that lasts forever."

Ephesians 5:5 "Be sure of this! No person who does sex sins or who is not pure will have any part in the holy nation of Christ and of God."

What things do you need to give up in order to honor God with your body?

____

____

____

____

____

____

____

____

Detox Day 17   Date:

Meditation Scriptures:

Galatians 6:6-7 "Do not be fooled. You cannot fool God. A man will get back whatever he plants! If a man does things to please his sinful old self, his soul will be lost. If a man does things to please the Holy Spirit, he will have life that lasts forever."

Ephesians 5:5 "Be sure of this! No person who does sex sins or who is not pure will have any part in the holy nation of Christ and of God."

What relationships do you need to set boundaries in to protect your purity?

____

____

____

What boundaries will you set in the relationships you listed above?

____

____

____

____

____

Detox Day 17
Date:

Meditation Scriptures:

Galatians 6:6-7 "Do not be fooled. You cannot fool God. A man will get back whatever he plants! If a man does things to please his sinful old self, his soul will be lost. If a man does things to please the Holy Spirit, he will have life that lasts forever."

Ephesians 5:5 "Be sure of this! No person who does sex sins or who is not pure will have any part in the holy nation of Christ and of God."

Write a list of any inappropriate content that you need to stop watching.

____

____

What will you do when you are tempted to watch the content you listed above?

____

____

____

____

Detox Day 17   Date:

Meditation Scriptures:

Galatians 6:6-7 "Do not be fooled. You cannot fool God. A man will get back whatever he plants! If a man does things to please his sinful old self, his soul will be lost. If a man does things to please the Holy Spirit, he will have life that lasts forever."

Ephesians 5:5 "Be sure of this! No person who does sex sins or who is not pure will have any part in the holy nation of Christ and of God."

Are there any sins you've committed against your body that you need to confess?

____

____

____

What temptations have you faced in your sexual purity today?

____

____

____

____

____

____

Detox Day 17

Date:

Meditation Scriptures:

Galatians 6:6-7 "Do not be fooled. You cannot fool God. A man will get back whatever he plants! If a man does things to please his sinful old self, his soul will be lost. If a man does things to please the Holy Spirit, he will have life that lasts forever."

Ephesians 5:5 "Be sure of this! No person who does sex sins or who is not pure will have any part in the holy nation of Christ and of God."

What victories did you experience today?

____

____

____

____

What is your biggest takeaway from today's meditation scripture and journaling?

____

____

____

____

Detox Day 17

Date:

Meditation Scriptures:

Galatians 6:6-7 "Do not be fooled. You cannot fool God. A man will get back whatever he plants! If a man does things to please his sinful old self, his soul will be lost. If a man does things to please the Holy Spirit, he will have life that lasts forever."

Ephesians 5:5 "Be sure of this! No person who does sex sins or who is not pure will have any part in the holy nation of Christ and of God."

Take time to write out your thoughts and prayers to God about your purity.

____
____
____
____
____
____
____
____
____

Detox Day 17   Date:

Meditation Scriptures:

Galatians 6:6-7 "Do not be fooled. You cannot fool God. A man will get back whatever he plants! If a man does things to please his sinful old self, his soul will be lost. If a man does things to please the Holy Spirit, he will have life that lasts forever."

Ephesians 5:5 "Be sure of this! No person who does sex sins or who is not pure will have any part in the holy nation of Christ and of God."

How do you feel about the conversation you had
with your detox partner/group today?

____

____

____

____

____

I want to encourage you that you made an amazing
and godly decision to persevere in your purity today.
Keep striving for godliness. God will strengthen you!
Keep Going!

  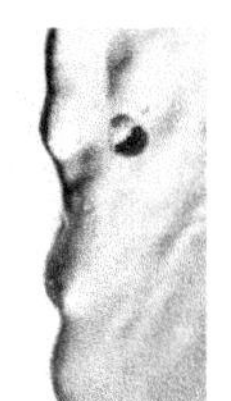

Detox Day 18   Date:

Meditation Scriptures:

Hebrews 13:4 "Marriage should be respected by everyone. God will punish those who do sex sins and are not faithful in marriage."

1st Corinthians 7:2 "But since sexual immorality is occurring, each man should have seuxal relations with his own wife, and each woman with her own husband"

What is God saying to you in today's meditation scriptures?

____

____

____

____

____

____

____

____

____

____

Detox Day 18   Date:

Meditation Scriptures:

Hebrews 13:4 "Marriage should be respected by everyone. God will punish those who do sex sins and are not faithful in marriage."

1st Corinthians 7:2 "But since sexual immorality is occurring, each man should have seuxal relations with his own wife, and each woman with her own husband"

What things do you need to give up in order to honor God with your body?

____

____

____

____

____

____

____

____

Detox Day 18   Date:

Meditation Scriptures:

Hebrews 13:4 "Marriage should be respected by everyone. God will punish those who do sex sins and are not faithful in marriage."

1st Corinthians 7:2 "But since sexual immorality is occurring, each man should have seuxal relations with his own wife, and each woman with her own husband"

What relationships do you need to set boundaries in to protect your purity?

____

____

____

What boundaries will you set in the relationships you listed above?

____

____

____

____

Detox Day 18   Date:

Meditation Scriptures:

Hebrews 13:4 "Marriage should be respected by everyone. God will punish those who do sex sins and are not faithful in marriage."

1st Corinthians 7:2 "But since sexual immorality is occurring, each man should have seuxal relations with his own wife, and each woman with her own husband"

Write a list of any inappropriate content that you need to stop watching.

____
____
____

____

What will you do when you are tempted to watch the content you listed above?

____
____
____
____
____

  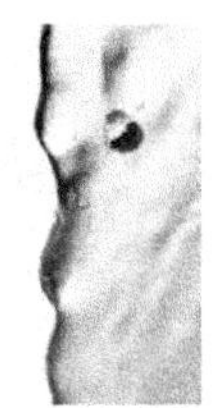

Detox Day 18   Date:

Meditation Scriptures:

Hebrews 13:4 "Marriage should be respected by everyone. God will punish those who do sex sins and are not faithful in marriage."

1st Corinthians 7:2 "But since sexual immorality is occurring, each man should have seuxal relations with his own wife, and each woman with her own husband"

Are there any sins you've committed against your body that you need to confess?

____

____

____

____

What temptations have you faced in your sexual purity today?

____

____

____

____

____

Detox Day 18   Date:

Meditation Scriptures:

Hebrews 13:4 "Marriage should be respected by everyone. God will punish those who do sex sins and are not faithful in marriage."

1st Corinthians 7:2 "But since sexual immorality is occurring, each man should have seuxal relations with his own wife, and each woman with her own husband"

What victories did you experience today?

____

____

____

What is your biggest takeaway from today's meditation scripture and journaling?

____

____

____

____

  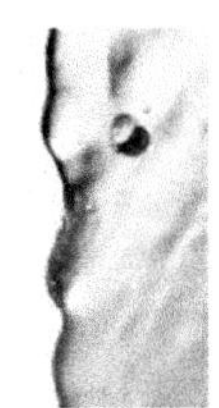

Detox Day 18   Date:

Meditation Scriptures:

Hebrews 13:4 "Marriage should be respected by everyone. God will punish those who do sex sins and are not faithful in marriage."

1st Corinthians 7:2 "But since sexual immorality is occurring, each man should have seuxal relations with his own wife, and each woman with her own husband"

Take time to write out your thoughts and prayers to God about your purity.

____
____
____
____
____
____
____
____
____

Detox Day 18   Date:

Meditation Scriptures:

Hebrews 13:4 "Marriage should be respected by everyone. God will punish those who do sex sins and are not faithful in marriage."

1st Corinthians 7:2 "But since sexual immorality is occurring, each man should have seuxal relations with his own wife, and each woman with her own husband"

How do you feel about the conversation you had with your detox partner/group today?

____
____
____
____
____
____

I want to encourage you that you made an amazing and godly decision to persevere in your purity today. Keep striving for godliness. God will strengthen you!
Keep Going!

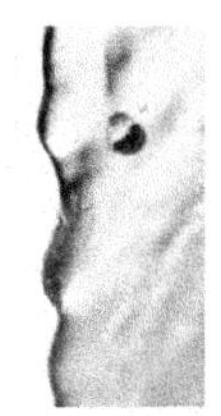

Detox Day 19   Date:

Meditation Scriptures:

1 Corinthians 6:13 "The body was not meant for sex sins. It was meant to work for the Lord."

2 Corinthians 7:1 "Since we have these great promises, dear friends, let us turn away from every sin of the body or of the spirit. Let us honor God with love and fear by giving ourselves to Him in every way."

What is God saying to you in today's meditation scriptures?

____
____
____
____
____
____
____
____
____
____

Detox Day 19   Date:

Meditation Scriptures:

1 Corinthians 6:13 "The body was not meant for sex sins. It was meant to work for the Lord."

2 Corinthians 7:1 "Since we have these great promises, dear friends, let us turn away from every sin of the body or of the spirit. Let us honor God with love and fear by giving ourselves to Him in every way."

What things do you need to give up in order to honor God with your body?

____

____

____

____

____

____

____

____

____

____

Detox Day 19   Date:

Meditation Scriptures:

1 Corinthians 6:13 "The body was not meant for sex sins. It was meant to work for the Lord."

2 Corinthians 7:1 "Since we have these great promises, dear friends, let us turn away from every sin of the body or of the spirit. Let us honor God with love and fear by giving ourselves to Him in every way."

What relationships do you need to set boundaries in to protect your purity?

____

____

____

What boundaries will you set in the relationships you listed above?

____

____

____

____

Detox Day 19

Date:

Meditation Scriptures:

1 Corinthians 6:13 "The body was not meant for sex sins. It was meant to work for the Lord."

2 Corinthians 7:1 "Since we have these great promises, dear friends, let us turn away from every sin of the body or of the spirit. Let us honor God with love and fear by giving ourselves to Him in every way."

Write a list of any inappropriate content that you need to stop watching.

____

____

____

What will you do when you are tempted to watch the content you listed above?

____

____

____

____

Detox Day 19   Date:

Meditation Scriptures:

1 Corinthians 6:13 "The body was not meant for sex sins. It was meant to work for the Lord."

2 Corinthians 7:1 "Since we have these great promises, dear friends, let us turn away from every sin of the body or of the spirit. Let us honor God with love and fear by giving ourselves to Him in every way."

Are there any sins you've committed against your body that you need to confess?

____

____

____

What temptations have you faced in your sexual purity today?

____

____

____

____

____

Detox Day 19   Date:

Meditation Scriptures:

1 Corinthians 6:13 "The body was not meant for sex sins. It was meant to work for the Lord."

2 Corinthians 7:1 "Since we have these great promises, dear friends, let us turn away from every sin of the body or of the spirit. Let us honor God with love and fear by giving ourselves to Him in every way."

What victories did you experience today?

____

____

____

____

What is your biggest takeaway from today's meditation scripture and journaling?

____

____

____

____

Detox Day 19   Date:

Meditation Scriptures:

1 Corinthians 6:13 "The body was not meant for sex sins. It was meant to work for the Lord."

2 Corinthians 7:1 "Since we have these great promises, dear friends, let us turn away from every sin of the body or of the spirit. Let us honor God with love and fear by giving ourselves to Him in every way."

Take time to write out your thoughts and prayers to God about your purity.

____

____

____

____

____

____

____

____

____

____

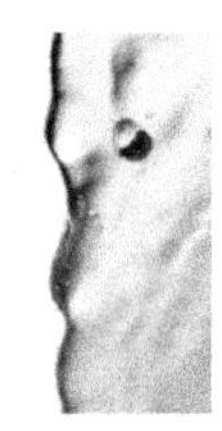

Detox Day 19   Date:

Meditation Scriptures:

1 Corinthians 6:13 "The body was not meant for sex sins. It was meant to work for the Lord."

2 Corinthians 7:1 "Since we have these great promises, dear friends, let us turn away from every sin of the body or of the spirit. Let us honor God with love and fear by giving ourselves to Him in every way."

How do you feel about the conversation you had
with your detox partner/group today?

____

____

____

____

____

____

I want to encourage you that you made an amazing
and godly decision to persevere in your purity today.
Keep striving for godliness. God will strengthen you!
Keep Going!

  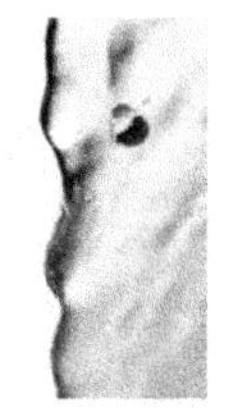

Detox Day 20   Date:

Meditation Scriptures:

Hebrews 2:1 2b "Let us put everything out of our lives that keeps us from doing what we should. Let us keep running in the race that God has planned for us. Let us keep looking to Jesus"

2 Timothy 2:22 "Turn away from the sinful things young people want to do. Go after what is right. Have a desire for faith and love and peace."

What is God saying to you in today's meditation scriptures?

____

____

____

____

____

____

____

____

____

Detox Day 20

Date:

Meditation Scriptures:

Hebrews 2:1 2b "Let us put everything out of our lives that keeps us from doing what we should. Let us keep running in the race that God has planned for us. Let us keep looking to Jesus"

2 Timothy 2:22 "Turn away from the sinful things young people want to do. Go after what is right. Have a desire for faith and love and peace."

What things do you need to give up in order to honor God with your body?

____

____

____

____

____

____

____

____

____

Detox Day 20

Date:

Meditation Scriptures:

Hebrews 2:1 2b "Let us put everything out of our lives that keeps us from doing what we should. Let us keep running in the race that God has planned for us. Let us keep looking to Jesus"

2 Timothy 2:22 "Turn away from the sinful things young people want to do. Go after what is right. Have a desire for faith and love and peace."

What relationships do you need to set boundaries in to protect your purity?

____

____

What boundaries will you set in the relationships you listed above?

____

____

____

____

Detox Day 20   Date:

Meditation Scriptures:

Hebrews 2:1 2b "Let us put everything out of our lives that keeps us from doing what we should. Let us keep running in the race that God has planned for us. Let us keep looking to Jesus"

2 Timothy 2:22 "Turn away from the sinful things young people want to do. Go after what is right. Have a desire for faith and love and peace."

Write a list of any inappropriate content that you need to stop watching.

____

____

____

What will you do when you are tempted to watch the content you listed above?

____

____

____

____

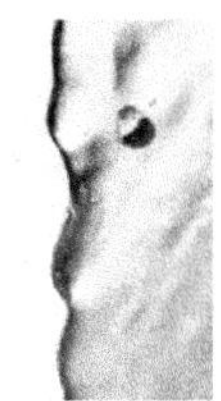

Detox Day 20   Date:

Meditation Scriptures:

Hebrews 2:1 2b "Let us put everything out of our lives that keeps us from doing what we should. Let us keep running in the race that God has planned for us. Let us keep looking to Jesus"

2 Timothy 2:22 "Turn away from the sinful things young people want to do. Go after what is right. Have a desire for faith and love and peace."

Are there any sins you've committed against your body that you need to confess?

____

____

____

What temptations have you faced in your sexual purity today?

____

____

____

____

____

Detox Day 20   Date:

Meditation Scriptures:

Hebrews 2:1 2b "Let us put everything out of our lives that keeps us from doing what we should. Let us keep running in the race that God has planned for us. Let us keep looking to Jesus"

2 Timothy 2:22 "Turn away from the sinful things young people want to do. Go after what is right. Have a desire for faith and love and peace."

What victories did you experience today?

____
____
____

____

What is your biggest takeaway from today's meditation scripture and journaling?

____
____
____
____

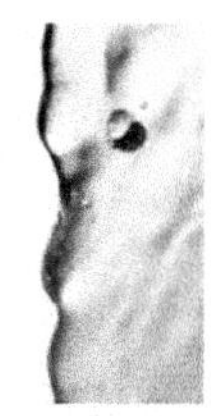

Detox Day 20   Date:

Meditation Scriptures:

Hebrews 2:1 2b "Let us put everything out of our lives that keeps us from doing what we should. Let us keep running in the race that God has planned for us. Let us keep looking to Jesus"

2 Timothy 2:22 "Turn away from the sinful things young people want to do. Go after what is right. Have a desire for faith and love and peace."

Take time to write out your thoughts and prayers to God about your purity.

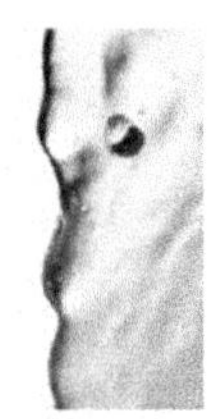

Detox Day 20   Date:

Meditation Scriptures:

Hebrews 2:1 2b "Let us put everything out of our lives that keeps us from doing what we should. Let us keep running in the race that God has planned for us. Let us keep looking to Jesus"

2 Timothy 2:22 "Turn away from the sinful things young people want to do. Go after what is right. Have a desire for faith and love and peace."

How do you feel about the conversation you had
with your detox partner/group today?

____

____

____

____

____

____

I want to encourage you that you made an amazing
and godly decision to persevere in your purity today.
Keep striving for godliness. God will strengthen you!
Keep Going!

Detox Day 21   Date:

Meditation Scriptures:

1 Peter 1:14-15 "Be like children who obey. Do not desire to sin like you used to when you did not know any better. Be holy in every part of your life. Be like the Holy One Who chose you."

1 Thessalonians 4:7 "For God has not called us to live in sin. He has called us to live a holy life."

What is God saying to you in today's meditation scriptures?

Detox Day 21

Date:

Meditation Scriptures:

1 Peter 1:14-15 "Be like children who obey. Do not desire to sin like you used to when you did not know any better. Be holy in every part of your life. Be like the Holy One Who chose you."

1 Thessalonians 4:7 "For God has not called us to live in sin. He has called us to live a holy life."

What things do you need to give up in order to honor God with your body?

____

____

____

____

____

____

____

____

____

Detox Day 21   Date:

Meditation Scriptures:

1 Peter 1:14-15 "Be like children who obey. Do not desire to sin like you used to when you did not know any better. Be holy in every part of your life. Be like the Holy One Who chose you."

1 Thessalonians 4:7 "For God has not called us to live in sin. He has called us to live a holy life."

What relationships do you need to set boundaries in to protect your purity?

____
____
____
____

What boundaries will you set in the relationships you listed above?

____
____
____
____

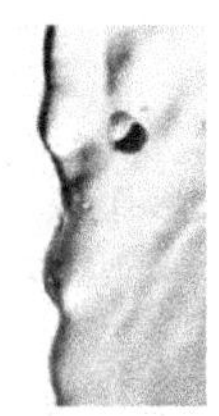

Detox Day 21

Date:

Meditation Scriptures:

1 Peter 1:14-15 "Be like children who obey. Do not desire to sin like you used to when you did not know any better. Be holy in every part of your life. Be like the Holy One Who chose you."

1 Thessalonians 4:7 "For God has not called us to live in sin. He has called us to live a holy life."

Write a list of any inappropriate content that you
need to stop watching.

____
____
____

What will you do when you are tempted to watch
the content you listed above?

____
____
____

Detox Day 21   Date:

Meditation Scriptures:

1 Peter 1:14-15 "Be like children who obey. Do not desire to sin like you used to when you did not know any better. Be holy in every part of your life. Be like the Holy One Who chose you."

1 Thessalonians 4:7 "For God has not called us to live in sin. He has called us to live a holy life."

Are there any sins you've committed against your body that you need to confess?

____

____

____

____

What temptations have you faced in your sexual purity today?

____

____

____

____

____

Detox Day 21

Date:

Meditation Scriptures:

1 Peter 1:14-15 "Be like children who obey. Do not desire to sin like you used to when you did not know any better. Be holy in every part of your life. Be like the Holy One Who chose you."

1 Thessalonians 4:7 "For God has not called us to live in sin. He has called us to live a holy life."

What victories did you experience today?

____

____

____

____

What is your biggest takeaway from today's meditation scripture and journaling?

____

____

____

____

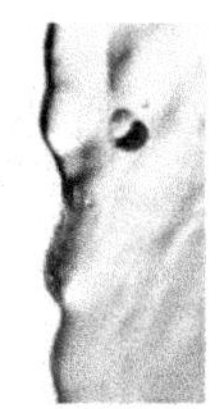

Detox Day 21

Date:

Meditation Scriptures:

1 Peter 1:14-15 "Be like children who obey. Do not desire to sin like you used to when you did not know any better. Be holy in every part of your life. Be like the Holy One Who chose you."

1 Thessalonians 4:7 "For God has not called us to live in sin. He has called us to live a holy life."

Take time to write out your thoughts and prayers to God about your purity.

Detox Day 21

Date:

Meditation Scriptures:

1 Peter 1:14-15 "Be like children who obey. Do not desire to sin like you used to when you did not know any better. Be holy in every part of your life. Be like the Holy One Who chose you."

1 Thessalonians 4:7 "For God has not called us to live in sin. He has called us to live a holy life."

How do you feel about the conversation you had
with your detox partner/group today?

I want to encourage you that you made an amazing
and godly decision to persevere in your purity today.
Keep striving for godliness. God will strengthen you!
Keep Going!

Chapter Ten
The Journey Continues

"I do not say that I have received this or have already become perfect. But I keep going on to make that life my own as Christ Jesus made me His own. No, Christian brothers, I do not have that life yet. But I do one thing. I forget everything that is behind me and look forward to that which is ahead of me."

PHILIPPIANS 3:12-13

You have now completed twenty-one days of this detox! I want to applaud you for persevering to this point. I hope that in the past three weeks you have gained a great understanding of God's call for you to be pure. Throughout the detox you have been practicing some of the most important spiritual disciplines. One of the most important disciplines you've practiced is reading and meditating on the word of God with intentionality daily. The only way for us to be transformed spiritually is by renewing our minds which requires studying the word of God consistently. Another discipline you have practiced is fasting. Fasting is key in our walk with God. When Jesus was talking to his disciples in Matthew chapter 6:16, he said "when you fast…". Jesus did not say "if you fast". Jesus' disciples were learning to imitate Jesus and Jesus himself practiced the discipline of fasting. You were also practicing confession and partnership during your detox. It is especially important for us to understand that we as people were not meant to do life alone. We especially were not meant to go through life in discipleship alone. Jesus himself said to his disciples, "love one another as I have loved you", in John 13:34. Loving one another involves looking out for each other spiritually like Jesus looked out for his disciples spiritually. Having a spiritual partner to whom you can confess your struggles, temptations, failures, and victories to as you go through life will help you grow and will keep you accountable in your purity. Journaling is also a very helpful practice you learned throughout the detox. Hopefully you learned the benefits of journaling throughout your detox journey. I encourage you to not stop journaling. Journaling will be very helpful for your lifelong journey of walking with God. The bible calls us to compare ourselves to Jesus and not to other people. When we are journaling daily as we walk with God, it helps us to have an honest view of how well we're imitating Christ instead of just going with the flow of what we see in other Christians. Continuing to practice all these disciplines is going to help you keep in step with repentance as your journey to purity continues.

Don't Look Back

When God delivered the Israelites from Egypt, he led them through the desert of testing and even though God had given them everything they needed they became discouraged in hard times, and they looked back for Egypt. This is the temptation of every human person on this earth! We are tempted to question the goodness of what God has done when we are faced with challenges. You will be faced with temptation as you continue in your journey for sexual purity. You will find yourself questioning whether all that you have gone through in this detox really helped you. You will feel weak at some point and Satan will try to tell you that you will never change!

Satan is waiting to mock you and the fact that you completed this detox. I have good news for you! Greater is he that is in you than he who is in the world! Do not look back! What you have deposited in your spirit, heart, and mind through completing this detox is already in you and it's up to you to keep it in and keep the contaminants of this world out. Don't let the enemy convince you that all of this was for nothing when he comes to tempt you in your purity. Your being tempted is not a sign of weakness, it's just a part of having this earthy body. Remember that even Jesus was tempted when he was in the desert, but he did not give in. In the garden of Gethsemane Jesus said the spirit is willing but the flesh is weak. Your spirit is willing too! Your willing spirit is what led you to set apart these last 21 days to focus on getting where God wants you to be in your purity. You desire to give God more! I encourage you to keep moving forward and no matter what the enemy tries DON'T LOOK BACK!

Keeping The Fervor

You have gotten pretty fired up and filled to the seams at this point if you followed the detox in full. You have been feasting on scriptures about sexual purity, you've been praying, fasting, meditating, and cleaning your "spiritual closet" out by confessing sin. I imagine you are pumped! If you did this detox with a group, you all have had some amazing fellowship and made some deep connections with each other! Now that the detox is over you might be wondering, "Now What?!". What will you do now to keep that fervor that you have? Well, I have more good news! That fire does not have to end here. You can keep that same fire for living in purity for God as you continue this journey through life.

The best way for you to keep your fervor is by practicing the same disciplines you have been practicing the last twenty-one days. You can also encourage yourself by sharing what you have learned with others. You can create your own sexual purity detox group. God can use you to help others and by leading them through this detox. God can use your group members to help you as well. Another way that you can keep the fervor is by purchasing *"**The Sexual Purity Detox - Forty Days of Fasting"*** journal. This journal is to help you continue your journey to sexual purity. *The Sexual Purity Detox - Forty*

Days of Fasting journal is full of scriptures for daily meditation and daily journal entries to help you continue detoxing your life of spiritual contaminants. My prayer is that in turn of completing this detox you are finding greater freedom in your sexual purity than you have ever experienced before! To God's glory!

Additional Scriptures

❖ **Isaiah 41:10** "So do not fear, for I am with you; do not be dismayed, for I am your God. I will strengthen you and help you; I will uphold you with my righteous right hand." Just so you know, you can"

❖ **Job 31:1** *"I have made a covenant with my eyes; Why then should I look upon a young woman?"*

❖ **Luke 9:23-24** *"Then He said to them all, 'If anyone desires to come after Me, let him deny himself, and take up his cross daily, and follow Me.'"*

❖ **Romans 6:1-2** *"What shall we say then? Shall we continue in sin that grace may abound? Certainly not! How shall we who died to sin live any longer in it?"*

❖ **Romans 6:12-13** *"Therefore do not let sin reign in your mortal body, that you should obey it in its lusts. And do not present your members as instruments of unrighteousness to sin, but present yourselves to God as being alive from the dead, and your members as instruments of righteousness to God."*

❖ **Romans 8:13** *"Therefore, brethren, we are debtors – not to the flesh, to live according to the flesh. For if you live according to the flesh you will die; but if by the Spirit you put to death the deeds of the body, you will live."*

❖ **1 Thessalonians 4:3** *"For this is the will of God, your sanctification: that you should abstain from sexual immorality."*

❖ **James 1:12** *"Blessed is the man who endures temptation; for when he has been approved, he will receive the crown of life which the Lord has promised to those who love Him."*

❖ **1 Peter 4:1-2** *"Therefore, since Christ suffered for us in the flesh, arm yourselves also with the same mind, for he who has suffered in the* *flesh has ceased from sin, that he no longer should live the rest of his time in the flesh for the lusts of men, but for the will of God."*

❖ **Galatians 5:16** "So I say, walk by the Spirit, and you will not gratify the desires of the flesh."

Printed in the USA
CPSIA information can be obtained
at www.ICGtesting.com
CBHW081519250824
13635CB00054B/889